W9-ACW-970

Guide To Pennsylvania Troops at Gettysburg

Guide To Pennsylvania Troops At Gettysburg

Richard Rollins and Dave Shultz

Rank and File Publications

1996

Publisher's Cataloging in Publication

Rollins, Richard M.
   Guide to Pennsylvania troops at
Gettysburg /   Richard M. Rollins, David
Shultz.
   p. cm.
   Includes bibliographical references.
   ISBN 0-9638993-6-8

   1. Gettysburg (Pa.), Battle of, 1863. 2.
Pennsylvania—History —Civil War, 1861-
1865—Regimental histories. 3. United
States—History—Civil War, 1861-1865—
Regimental Histories. I. Shultz, David. II.
Title.

E475.53.R65 1996   973.7'4'748

Preface

For many years, the story of Colonel Strong Vincent and the 83rd Pennsylvania Infantry at Gettysburg has been a source of inspiration for me and my family. My wife, Michele, has taken a special interest in preserving the memory and memorabilia of these courageous soldiers whose heroic defense of Little Round Top has become legendary.

Generations of Pennsylvanians also have taken pride in the service and sacrifice of the nearly 25,000 men from our state who participated in the battle. They came from every county and from every city and hamlet. Of the 79 Pennsylvania regiments that appeared at Gettysburg, many suffered terrible losses. The 151st, for example, registered 337 casualties—dead, wounded, and missing—the third highest total of all units, North and South, that fought during that fateful week in July, 1863.

Gettysburg has been recognized as the defining moment of the Civil War, a conflict that has been called the defining moment in American history. President Lincoln instantly understood the significance of the battle and chose the dedication of the National Cemetery at Gettysburg to deliver his magnificent address that articulated the ultimate meaning of our national experience.

Pennsylvania's presence at Gettysburg is symbolized today by the state memorial, where visitors can read the names of the dead and wounded from each regiment. They can look out over the heart of the battlefield and imagine the carnage of the conflict. They can walk out onto the fields and read the inscriptions on hundreds of regimental monuments and listen to the guided tours by park rangers and battlefield guides. these stories continue to have the same enduring power as they did over 130 years ago. In recent years, new sources of information have allowed historians to tell new stories about the ordinary soldiers as well as their leaders. We should take every advantage to make these stories available to new audiences and to preserve their unique legacy.

Governor Tom Ridge
Harrisburg
February, 1996

Table of Contents

Introduction..xi

July 1st...1

   Map I: Seminary &. Oak Ridges.....................1

   26th Militia...3

   Bell's Cavalry Company..................................4

   17th Cavalry...6

   56th Infantry..7

   121st Infantry..8

   142nd Infantry...11

   151st Infantry...12

   Battery B, 1st Light Artillery(Cooper's).....16

   149th Infantry..18

   150th Infantry..21

   143rd Infantry..23

   11th Infantry...26

   88th Infantry..28

   90th Infantry..30

   107th Infantry...31

   74th Infantry..32

   Map II: North Field &. Town...................33

   75th Infantry..34

   153rd Infantry..35

   27th Infantry..36

   73rd Infantry..37

July 2nd...39

   Map III: South Field...................................40

   99th Infantry...41

   110th Infantry...42

   118th Infantry...15

   62nd Infantry..46

   83rd Infantry..51

   91st Infantry...52

   155th Infantry...53

   81st Infantry...54

   148th Infantry...56

116th Infantry..57
140th Infantry..61
53rd Infantry..63
145th Infantry..65
26th Infantry..66
11th Reserves..67
1st Reserves..69
2nd Reserves..70
5th Reserves..72
6th Reserves..74
139th Infantry..75
93rd Infantry..76
98th Infantry..77
95th Infantry..79
96th Infantry..80
9th Reserves..81
10th Reserves..82
119th Infantry..82
68th Infantry..83
Map IV: Peach Orchard..85
63rd Infantry..87
141st Infantry..88
Ind. Batt. C & F (Thompson's)............................91
57th Infantry..93
105th Infantry..95
114th Infantry..98
69th Infantry..101
Map V: Cemetery Ridge..102
71st Infantry..103
72nd Infantry..105
106th Infantry..106
121st Infantry..109
88th Infantry..111
90th Infantry..112
107th Infantary..112
1st Cavalry..113
2nd Cavalry..114
4th Cavalry..115
6th Cavalry..116
Batt. B., 1st Lt. Artillery(Cooper's)............................117
Batts. F &. G., 1st Artillery(Rickett's)............................118
Map VI: Culp's Hill, etc..119
Ind. Batt. E(Knap's)..121
27th Infantry..123
73rd Infantry..125
56th Infantry..125
109th Infantry..126

29th Infantry...127
28th Infantry...130
147th Infantry...131
46th Infantry...133
74th Infantry...135
75th Infantry...135

July 3rd...**137**

Map VII: South &. East Cavalry Fields........138
82nd Infantry...139
111th Infantry.. 140
109th Infantry..143
28th Infantry..142
23rd Infantry..143
147th Infantry..144
56th Infantry..144
46th Infantry..145
29th Infantry..146
Batts. F &. G, 1st Lt. Artillery(Rickett's).........146
Batt. H, 3rd Heavy Artillery(Rank's)................147
151st Infantry...147
69th Infantry..148
71st Infantry..149
106th Infantry..150
72nd Infantry...151
99th Infantry..153
114th Infantry..154
141st Infantry..156
121st Infantry..157
143rd Infantry..157
150th Infantry..157
57th Infantry..159
145th Infantry..159
140th Infantry..160
88th Infantry..161
107th Infantry..163
110th Infantry..162
2nd Cavalry...163
1st Cavalry..163
115th Infantry..164
Batt. B, 1st Lt. Artillery(Cooper's)....................164
119th Infantry..165
118th Infantry..165
139th Infantry..165
93rd Infantry..166

102nd Infantry...166
11th Reserves..167
1st Reserves...168
2nd Reserves...168
9th Reserves...169
10th Reserves..169
27th Infantry..170
3rd Cavalry..170
61st Infantry..171
Ind. Battery E(Atwell's)...............................172
49th Infantry..173
16th Cavalry...173
6th Cavalry..174
18th Cavalry...174

Select Bibliography.................................**176**
Pennsylvania Medal of Honor Winners...........**178**

Guide To Pennsylvania Troops at Gettysburg

The best way to learn about a Civil War battlefield and the experiences of the men who fought there is to visit the battlefield in person, to walk over it tracing the movements and engagements of an individual or unit. Anyone interested in finding the places where an ancestor or a member of a home town unit marched and fought should begin by reading the secondary studies of that battle. But then it is imperative to get out and find those spots where important events occurred, see what they look like now and try to understand what they looked like then. That is the only way to truly comprehend a battle and an individual's experience in it.

Visitors often come to Gettysburg in search of information about a certain unit and their experiences at Gettysburg, usually men from their home town, county or state. **Guide to Pennsylvania Troops at Gettysburg** is designed to help the reader find the locations and follow the paths of individuals—be they officers or enlisted men—and the units in which they served. It is meant to offer a simple yet comprehensive set of unit profiles that would give the reader a basic introduction to each Pennsylvania unit that fought at Gettysburg, along with maps and photographs that would assist the reader in finding the places they want to see.

In order to keep this book as inexpensive as possible, we decided to draw the line at units, and not add more information about individuals. Pennsylvania was blessed with some of the finest performances by officers during the war, but to add sufficient information about all of them would have added many pages and photographs, a significant amount of preparation time, and an increase in the price of the book. Anyone interested in Major General George G. Meade, commander of the Army of the Potomac, or Major Generals and corps commanders Winfield S. Hancock, John Reynolds and O. O. Howard, or Brigadier Generals Samuel Crawford, Alexander Hays, John Gibbon, John Buford or many others at the brigade level, should begin with the secondary sources cited below.

We strongly recommend that a reader first become

familiar with at least one general history of the battle, such as Glenn Tucker's **High Tide At Gettysburg**. It is also best to read one of the major studies of the part of the battle in which the unit that you are interested in fought. For the first day, see David Martin, **Gettysburg: July 1st**. For the second day see either Harry Pfanz, **Gettysburg: The Second Day** for the south end of the field or Harry Pfanz, **Gettysburg: Culp's Hill and Cemetery Hill** for the north end. While there is no comprehensive and detailed study of all activity on July 3rd, one should be familiar with George Stewart, **Pickett's Charge: A Microhistory of the Final Attack At Gettysburg, July 3, 1863**, if the unit you are interested in participated in that attack.

On June 26th, 1863, the 26th Pennsylvania State Emergency Volunteer Regiment (Home Guard) became the first organized Federal unit to skirmish with organized units from the Army of Northern Virginia near the Adams County seat of Gettysburg. Seven days later on the sweltering afternoon of July 3rd, the 18th Pennsylvania Cavalry participated in a desperate but futile charge against strong enemy positions posted in the woods below Big Round Top, near the point where West Confederate Avenue now crosses Plum Run. The charge by the 18th, commonly known as Farnsworth's Charge, was the last large-scale combat at the battle of Gettysburg.

Between the engagements of the 26th Militia and the repulse of the 18th Cavalry, 79 Pennsylvania units made their appearance at Gettysburg. Most of these units were veteran infantry and cavalry regiments or artillery batteries with considerable experience in combat before the Gettysburg Campaign. Others had no combat experience, and would "see the elephant" for the first time.

The small company commanded by Captain Robert Bell, for example, was a make shift company of irregular militia, formed around a nucleus of six veteran soldiers from the recently disbanded 21st Pennsylvania Cavalry. Although they did not participate in the main battle, they helped the cause by delaying Ewell's advance toward York, as well as by setting fire to the bridge over the Susquehanna River at Wrightsville. One of their number was killed in action on June 26th near the Nathaniel Lightener house located on the Baltimore Pike.

The Commonwealth of Pennsylvania supplied at

least 24,412 men, militia included, to the battle of Gettysburg. These men came from all 66 counties in the state. They were city-bred merchants and educators from Philadelphia and Harrisburg; miners and factory workers from Johnstown and Reading; backwoodsmen and river men from Erie and Pittsburgh. The majority were simple farmers and laborers, fighting that much harder to clear their state of an unfriendly and invading foreign power threatening their families and way of life.

The involvement of Pennsylvania units varied considerably. During the battle 741 Pennsylvanians were killed in action, another 3,762 suffered wounds, and 1,384 were captured by the Confederates. The total loss of all Pennsylvania troops at Gettysburg came to 5,887, or 24.1 percent of all those present for action. Some units were not actively engaged in combat, thus the percentage of casualties of men actively engaged is actually higher. Pennsylvania ranked 12th out of 15 states in total percentage of casualties, and second in actual numbers killed, wounded, and missing. The 23rd Volunteer Regiment was extremely large but did almost no fighting. Out of 538 men, one was killed and 13 suffered wounds. On July 3rd, this unit was moved about the field and placed in reserve positions before its combat in previously built entrenched positions on Culp's Hill. The 151st, on the other hand, suffered so terribly that its aggregate 337 casualties amounted to the third largest number of all regiments engaged during the battle, behind the 26th North Carolina and 24th Michigan.

Of Pennsylvania's 741 dead, 528 are buried in the Soldiers National Cemetery, 18 in Evergreen Cemetery and eight in York Memorial Cemetery. At least one-fourth of these are unidentified. Many of the remaining 195 dead were removed by their families to private lots throughout the state. Many of the 3,762 wounded eventually died from their wounds, or from disease associated with their wounds, within a few months after the battle. Some carried the scars and other complications from wounds inflicted during the battle for many years after the war ended, and succumbed to them later in life.

Of the 1,384 missing, approximately one-half never found their way back home. Many of these men died in prisoner of war camps scattered throughout the South. The total missing also includes an unknown number of men who were vaporized on the battlefield, never to be seen again. It also includes the men whose bodies were mistakenly interred in unmarked mass Confederate graves. The exact number of Pennsylvanians who lost their lives as a result of their service at Gettysburg will never be known.

Guide to Pennsylvania Troops at Gettysburg is divided in chronological fashion, one chapter for each of the three days. Appendixes contain additional information: a short bibliography for those interested in reading more, and some information on Pennsylvania men who were awarded the Congressional Medal of Honor for their efforts on this field.

* Each chapter begins with a map that shows the location of the unit's participation. It includes the major landmarks and the site of the unit's monument.

* The first unit to become engaged in actual combat is presented first, followed by all others engaged on that day in the approximate order of their appearance.

* In July of 1863 the Army of the Potomac included approximately 93,000 fighting men, or "effectives," as a healthy, fully equipped individual soldier was called in the military jargon of the day. It was commanded by Major General George Gordon Meade, a son of the Keystone state, who had replaced Major General Joseph Hooker just a few days before the battle. The infantry was divided into seven **Corps**, averaging about 10,000 men. Each Corps had two or more (normally three) **Divisions,** usually numbering between 3,000 and 6,000 men each. Each division had two or more **Brigades**, numbering about 1,000 to 2,000 men each.

* Each brigade contained four or more **Regiments**, and that is the level with which this book is primarily concerned. Military commanders at Gettysburg used the brigade as the fundamental tactical unit. The Union army, unlike the Confederate army, normally put regiments together in brigades without reference to their state of origin. Thus it was common for a Pennsylvania regiment to serve in the brigade with two or three other regiments from different states.

* Each entry is a basic profile of the unit and its experiences during the battle. The entry has three parts.

1) A photograph of the unit's monument. This photo

is intended to help the reader identify the site of the monument, with the assumption that the unit's action took place near the monument. The photo is *not* intended to allow the reader to read the inscriptions on the monument. In addition, one should be very careful in evaluating a monument or relying on it for information. The monuments were designed and inscriptions written generally between 1880 and 1913, when the veterans were involved in memorializing themselves, by people hired by the men of the regiment, or by individuals appointed by the state. There is *no correlation* between the size or elaborateness of a monument and the significance of their actions during the battle. The 8th Cavalry, for example, has a large and ornate monument on Cemetery Ridge, but in fact that had only one man at Gettysburg during the battle, and he was assigned to Headquarters as a courier. Just a few yards north of that, the 84th Infantry has a very impressive monument. They had 10 men in the battle.

Furthermore, the site of each monument must be carefully considered in relation to the unit's actions. The Gettysburg Battlefield Memorial Association, the organization that supervised the placement of many (but not all) of the monuments, attempted to have the monuments placed approximately where the action occurred, and when the unit moved frequently, at its most advanced position. They were not always successful. The 147th Pennsylvania, a regiment that was fiercely engaged on Culp's Hill, has a large and ornate monument on Round Top, marking the spot where they merely bivouacked, and were not engaged, on July 1st. A few regiments have two or even three monuments, and each must be carefully evaluated.

2) A database of basic information about the unit. This is a "snapshot" of the unit and its history, and will give the reader interested in a specific unit some essential information: its location in the chain of command of the Army of the Potomac, its Corps, Division, Brigade; where the men were raised, where and when the unit was organized, the name(s) of the leaders during the battle, what weapons they carried and the extent of their casualties.

Unit: gives the designation.

Other Name: many of the units were originally raised for a certain purpose, such as home guard, or service in a specific circumstance, and were later given a designation as part of the state's troops.

Organization: the unit's location in the chain of command. It is hoped the reader can use this information to develop an understand of how the unit's actions related to those of others in its brigade, division or corps.

Raised: where the men lived when they signed up.

Mustered: a unit was "mustered" when it was formally sworn into the service.

Commander: the names of the men who led the unit at Gettysburg, the years of their birth and death. When one died or was promoted at Gettysburg, the name of his successor is given.

Monument Location: where the monument can be found.

Map: the map on which the unit can be found.

Strength: the number of men the unit had at the beginning of the battle.

Losses: the number reported **K**illed, **W**ounded, or **M**issing.

Weapons: the type of gun they carried. **.58**, etc., refers to the size of the bullets they fired. **Austrian**, etc., refers to the country from which they were imported. **Springfield** refers to a gun manufactured by the U.S. government. The main factory was in Springfield, Massachusetts, but a significant portion of the guns so designated were made by contractors at other locations, using the same patterns.

The heart of the database is the **Summary** of their activities. It is designed to let the reader follow the unit's actions on a certain day. Those movements are described using modern landmarks on the battlefield, to aid the reader in following their development. In cases in which a unit participated on more than one day, the second entry refers the reader to the earlier entry for the basic information. The reader should be aware that when we describe the movements of troops via the West Confederate Avenue, Hancock Avenue, etc., that those roads did not exist in 1863, let alone as the nicely paved thoroughfares we drive on today.

3) The third part of each entry is the story of the units' experiences told in their officer's own words in their post-battle accounts. During the Civil War the ranking officer of each regiment provided its brigade commander with a written report detailing its activity during a certain period of time. Those reports were used by the brigade commander to write a brigade report that was passed to the division commander. The same was true at the division and corps level, and the army commander used these to write his own report to the Secretary of War. In the 1880s the U. S. Government gathered as many of these "official reports" as they could locate and published them in 128 volumes as **The War of the Rebellion: Official Records of the Union and Confederate Armies** (Washington, D.C.: United States Government Printing Office, 1880-1901), commonly referred to as the **Official Records**, or simply as the **OR**. Not all units turned in reports after Gettysburg, and some that were written were not included in this collection. When available, they provide an invaluable source for the student of the war. We have included as many of the reports as possible, edited to highlight the unit's action during the three days at Gettysburg. If a unit was active on just one day, but had other activities on the other days, such as guarding prisoners or waiting in reserve, we have included the additional material in the report for the day of their most significant action. If no report is included it is because it did not appear in the **Official Records**, or because the report that is included shed no light on their activities on the day under consideration.

    * Finally, we need to alert the reader that the battlefield that you are going to walk over is not exactly the same terrain that the soldiers fought upon. The Gettysburg battlefield has changed since 1863, and in some ways the alterations in the landscape have been very dramatic. While this is true all over the battlefield, we cannot describe every change that has occurred since 1863. Two obvious cases will demonstrate the extent of the changes and how the interested visitor must take them into consideration. The first time one stands at the Angle and looks west to view the fields of Pickett's Charge, it is easy to imagine the Confederate lines emerging from the woods directly across the valley near the Virginia monument, and marching in a perfect line straight at you. In fact, this imagined scene is wrong in almost every respect. No troops emerged from that area. Instead there were two wings, one beginning 200 or more yards south of the monument, the other about the same distance north. If you stand at the Angle, you cannot see the area where most of Pickett's Virginia Division began their

march. As they moved across the fields, they descended into several swales and could not be seen by the Union troops near the Angle, and at almost any point that Union infantry occupied on Cemetery Ridge, one or the other wings of the Confederate attack, or both, disappeared. In fact, there is almost no flat land between the two ridges. Much of this land was used to train tank drivers after World War I. No one apparently knows the extent of any alteration to the landscape that might have occurred during this period. A good portion of Pettigrew's and Trimble's divisions passed over land that is now part of a housing development built in the 1950s on what had been fields dedicated to agricultural crops south of the town. If you turn around and look east from the Angle, the slope up Cemetery Ridge to the Cyclorama building has also been significantly altered in the process of constructing that building.

An even more dramatic change has occurred on Cemetery Hill. From the western brow of the hill, in the vicinity of the current speaker's rostrum just across the Taneytown Road from the Visitor Center, Federal cannon were massed close together, and benefited from a spectacular view of the entire town and the fields to its north and south. It is difficult, if not impossible, to see the battlefield through the trees, and what one can see is the work of modern economic development: houses and commercial buildings. Yet in 1863 no trees blocked the view of Federal gunners who occupied the hill. Very few buildings existed between the Hill and the fields south of it, and none of those buildings blocked their view. Today it is difficult to imagine just how dominant the Cemetery Hill artillery positions were in 1863. When the visitor walks from the Visitor Center into the Soldiers' Cemetery, the trees planted on the western brow of the hill give one the illusion that the land is level, or close to it. The view that existed in 1863 has essentially disappeared, and our understanding of the actions that took place in 1863 is thereby diminished.

And so it goes throughout the entire battlefield. One need only read a superb book, William A. Frassanito's **Early Photography at Gettysburg**, to understand this point and how important it is. When we read Frassanito's book, after having spent countless hours going over the field over several decades, we felt as though we were seeing the battlefield for the first time.

At Gettysburg

The alterations in the landscape of the battlefield of Gettysburg have not stopped. Recently, the railroad cut just north of Gettysburg College was destroyed to make way for an improved railroad track bed. It seems that there are always developers actively seeking to destroy the hallowed ground where our ancestors shed their blood in defense of our liberty. The battlefield of Gettysburg is constantly threatened in this manner, and needs the support and effort of every person interested in the events that occurred there. Battlefield preservation has been an on going struggle since 1863, and this will continue throughout our lifetime.

Rich Rollins
Dave Shultz
Redondo Beach, California
January 27, 1996

July 1st

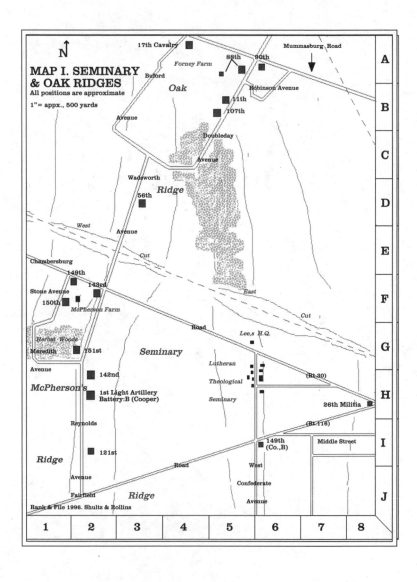

UNIT: 26th Militia. **OTHER NAME:** "26th Emergency Infantry Regiment," "Home Guard".

ORGANIZATION: State of Pennsylvania, Dept. of the Susquehanna.

ORGANIZED: From the counties of Adams, Chester, Columbia, Cumberland, Dauphin, Delaware, Franklin, Juniata, Lancaster, Lebanon, Montour, Perry, Susquehanna, and York. **M.I.** Camp Curtin & Camp Simmons, Harrisburg, June 21-24, 1863.

COMMANDER: Lt. Col. William W. Jennings.

MONUMENT LOCATION: A beautiful bronze statue located at the intersection of Rt. 30 (Chambersburg Pike) and South Middle Street approx. 1/2 mile west of the town diamond. 2) Small marker west of Marsh Creek on Rt. 30. No photo. **Map:** I, I-7 & II, H-2.

STRENGTH: 14 Cos, 746 effectives. **LOSSES:** K-0, W-26, M-176. Total: 202. Percent Loss: 16.2. The total numbered missing reflects the number paroled, and not those who turned up later after the battle of Gettysburg. The number of missing was surely much higher.

WEAPONS: .58 Springfields & Austrian, .577 Enfields, .69 Rifled & Smoothbores.

SUMMARY: On June 26th the 26th Militia moved several miles west of Gettysburg toward Belmont Schoolhouse Ridge, and deployed in line of battle. On sighting advanced mounted Confederates from White's 35th Virginia Battalion of cavalry, Col. Jennings ordered the 26th back. Retreated by column through town leaving supplies and ordnance at the train depot. Many men captured in rear guard action.

3

Reformed in line of battle east of Rock Creek along the road to Hunterstown to meet White's cavalry. Repulsed numerous cavalry charges while slowly moving northeast toward Hunterstown. Inflicted the first Confederate casualties at Gettysburg, and slowed Ewell's move toward York. Routed after a small engagement near Hunterstown, again with White's battalion, losing more captured and two dozen wounded. Reformed and continued north along the Old Harrisburg Road (Old Route 15). Heavy rain delayed White from pursuing, allowing Jennings to out-distance the veteran cavalry unit.

Skirmished again near Franklintown, again losing men missing in action. Returned to the retreat, continued north toward Harrisburg. Again skirmished, with reinforced support, near today's Township of Lemoyne, just across the river from Harrisburg. Jennings slipped away and moved across the river into Harrisburg and prepared to help defend the capital. Many men missing were hidden along the retreat by loyal citizens. Many other militiamen simply slipped off to return home. Ewell hastily paroled all captured militia on June 28-29, telling them to go home.

UNIT: Bell's Pennsylvania Cavalry Company. **OTHER NAME:** "21st Cavalry".

ORGANIZATION: State of Pennsylvania, Dept. of the Susquehanna.

ORGANIZED: From the counties of Adams, Cumberland, Chester, Dauphin, Franklin, Lancaster, Lebanon, Mifflin, Montgomery, Philadelphia, and York. **MUSTERED:** Camp Curtin, Harrisburg, and Philadelphia, June 21, 1863.

COMMANDER: Capt. Robert Bell.

MONUMENT LOCATION: Two on the east side of the Baltimore Pike, approx. 200 yards south of Colgrove Ave., across from Powers Hill. **Map:** VI, H-4.

STRENGTH: 1 Co., 76 effectives. **LOSSES:** K-1, W-9, M-2. Total: 12. Percent Loss: 9.1.

WEAPONS: Sharps and Burnside Carbines. Colt .44 revolvers.

SUMMARY: Recruited from volunteers who were already at Harrisburg for the purpose of mustering into a unit. Made up from a small nucleus of veterans from the 21st Cavalry and militia-trained youngsters from the immediate boroughs surrounding Gettysburg. Moved into town on the evening of June 25th, picketing all the roads north, east, and south of town. The 21st was given the task of moving west toward Chambersburg to reconnoiter as far as Cashtown. Moved back into Gettysburg after spotting advanced rebel cavalry along the Chambersburg Pike. Posted vedettes throughout the community on the morning of the 26th to cover the approaches to town. Accompanying Capt. Bell was Maj. C. M. Knox, adjutant to Maj. G.O. Haller, commanding officer of the District of Susquehanna. On Maj. Knox's request, most of Bell's cavalry company pulled back amid light skirmishing as the 26th Militia also withdrew. Successfully covered the flanks of the 26th Militia as that unit pulled back on the railroad grading through town.

One squad of vedettes failed to get the order to pull back as the 21st and 26th withdrew east of town. Posted on the Baltimore Pike near the Nathaniel Lightener house, south of the Evergreen Cemetery. Corporal George Sandoe sat on his horse talking with Daniel Lightener, son of Nathaniel, when some of White's mounted men approached, demanding their surrender. Sandoe fired at them and the rebels returned fire, hitting Sandoe in the head, and scattering his three comrades. Daniel Lightener was captured. Sandoe lay dying in the Baltimore Pike, a mere two miles from his home. This was the first Federal fatality at Gettysburg.

UNIT: 17th Cavalry (Co's D & H detached with V Corps Headquarters, Company K to the XI Corp). **OTHER NAME:** "162nd Volunteers".

ORGANIZATION: Cavalry Corps, 1st Div., 2nd Brig.

ORGANIZED: From the counties of Beaver, Bradford, Cumberland, Lancaster, Lebanon, Luzerne, Susquehanna, & Wayne. **MUSTERED:** Camp Simmons, Harrisburg, Oct. 18, 1862.

COMMANDER: Col. Josiah H. Kellogg (1836-1919).

MONUMENT LOCATION: On the Forney farm site, at the intersection of Buford Ave. and the Mummasburg Rd., West Oak Ridge. **Map:** I, A-4.

STRENGTH: 10 Cos, 464 effectives, **LOSSES:** K-0, W-0, C-4. Total: 4. Percent Loss: 0.9.

WEAPONS: Merrill & Smith Carbines, Colt .44s.

SUMMARY: Arrived at Gettysburg with brigade on the afternoon of June 30. Sent to Oak Ridge to picket the Mummasburg Road and surrounding countryside. Headquarters made in the John Forney barn adjacent to the Mummasburg Road. Vedettes west of Herr Ridge made contact with the enemy on the morning of July 1st when Confederate foragers fired on them. The regiment was mustered together and helped hold back the initial Confederate attacks. Vedettes from the 17th were also engaged in small arms fire with advanced enemy units moving south from both the Biglerville and Carlisle Pikes. Relieved by troops of the I Corps on their arrival, the 17th moved off Oak Ridge, continuing to cover the roads from the north, now including the Old Harrisburg Road. Forced back by overpowering numbers, they moved south to the Hanover Road east of town. Helped to cover the withdrawal of the XI Corps as it was swept from the fields north of town. Retreated to Cemetery Hill via the Henry Culp Farm. Moved with Devin's brigade to the Sherfy Peach Orchard to cover the army's left flank. Pulled out with Buford's division on the morning of the 2nd and moved south to Emmitsburg. Not actively engaged on July 2nd or 3rd.

UNIT: 56th Infantry, (Co E. detached). **OTHER NAME:** None.

ORGANIZATION: I Corps, 1st Div., 2nd Brig.

ORGANIZED: From the Counties of Centre, Indiana, Luzerne, Susquehanna & Philadelphia. **MUSTERED:** Camp Curtin, Harrisburg, on March 7, 1862.

COMMANDER: Col. John W. Hoffman (1824-1902).

MONUMENT LOCATION: On the east side of Wadsworth Ave., 1/4 mile north of Chambersburg Pike, also known today as Buford Ave. The monument represents the regiment's occupation on Oak Ridge, not its most advanced position. **Map:** I, E-4.

STRENGTH: 9 Cos, 252 effectives. **LOSSES:** K-14, W-61, M-55. Total: 130. Percentage Loss: 51.6.

WEAPONS: .58 Springfields.

SUMMARY: Arrived near Gettysburg in the forenoon leading the 1st Division, I Corps to Seminary Ridge. Advanced north, past the Lutheran Theological Seminary toward the Chambersburg Pike loading on the double-quick. Crossed north of the Pike and unfinished Railroad grading, moving into line of battle. Reportedly fired the first Federal infantry shot at Gettysburg as it collided with Davis's Mississippi Brigade. Stopping the Confederate movement east, the 56th and other regiments held their ground until flanked and forced back. Turning about, the regiment held its ground on east Oak Ridge near its monument. Withdrew due to overpowering numbers attacking from the right and front. Retreated through town in good order, turning about on several occasions to check the enemy, moved to Cemetery Hill.

Report of Col. J. William Hoffmann, Fifty-sixth Pennsylvania Infantry. IN THE FIELD, July 11, 1863.

CAPTAIN: On the morning of the 1st the regiment under my command left camp on the Emmitsburg and Gettysburg road, near Marsh Creek. We marched to Gettysburg, and engaged the enemy at 11 a. m. We suffered severely. In twenty minutes our loss in killed and wounded was over 70. On the 2d instant, we engaged the enemy on the ridge in rear of the town. My officers and men did all that could be asked of brave men. Of the enlisted men it is but just to mention Corporal [Patrick] Burns, of Company D, acting color-bearer, who was wounded while gallantly waving the flag in the face of the enemy on the evening of the 2nd instant. Private [George] Nolter, of Company D, was successful in capturing a major of the rebel army on the morning of the 4th instant.

Of the officers wounded, Lieutenant Gordon, Company B, has since died.

UNIT: 121st Infantry (Co. B detached).
OTHER NAME: None.

ORGANIZATION: I Corps, 3rd Div., 1st Brig.

ORGANIZED: From the counties of Philadelphia and Venango. **MUS-TERED:** Camp Knox, Philadelphia, Sept. 1, 1862.

COMMANDER: 1) Maj. Alexander Biddle (1819-1899). 2) Col. Chapman Biddle (1822-1880), returned to regiment from temporary brigade command on July 1st.

MONUMENT LOCATION: Reynolds Ave., 1/4 mile north of the Fairfield Road, on the crest of south McPherson Ridge.

This monument is for reference only. The first position occupied by the regiment was approx. 150 yards farther west on brow (military crest) of ridge. **Map:** I, J-3.

STRENGTH: 9 Cos, 262 effectives. **LOSSES:** K-12, W-106, M-61. Total: 179. Percent Loss: 68.1.

WEAPONS: .58 Springfields.

SUMMARY: Arrived with the 1st Brigade near noon from direction of Marsh Creek. Moved into line of battle north of present monument in support of Cooper's Pennsylvania battery. Moved southwest to a position several hundred yards west of their monument to the brow of south McPherson Ridge, anchoring the left flank of the I Corps. Supported the 80th New York as that regiment crossed to the west of Willoughby Run in a vain attempt to dislodge enemy infantry and sharpshooters. Retired back to the top of McPherson Ridge near present monument, and met several enemy charges before being flanked and swept from the field. Reorganized in swale between Seminary and McPherson Ridges. Withdrew to Seminary Ridge contesting each foot of retreat. Last position was left of the main Seminary building in support of Breck's Battery L. First New York Light Artillery. Retreated through open fields skirting the south edge of town to Cemetery Ridge.

Reports of Lieut. Col. Alexander Biddle, One hundred and twenty-first Pennsylvania Infantry. BIVOUAC IN THE FIELD, Thursday, July 2, 1863.

COLONEL: On arriving at the top of the hill bordering the valley in which Gettysburg lies, we were marched into a field on the left of a wood, through which we saw the First Division driving the enemy. We remained in this field, exposed at all times to an enfilading or direct fire, sometimes facing northwardly and sometimes westwardly, as the attack of the enemy varied. A large body of the enemy's troops had been seen to the west of our position throughout the day. While we were taking up a position facing to the north, to support a battery at the corner of a wood, the troops were seen advancing. We were ordered to form to meet them, and changed front to effect it. As the proper position assigned to the One hundred and twenty-first Regiment was immediately in front of the battery, we were moved to the extreme left, with the Twentieth New York on our right. I saw the line of the enemy slowly approaching up the hill, extending far beyond our left flank, for which we had no defense. As the enemy's faces appeared over the crest of the hill, we fired effectually into them, and, soon after, received a crushing fire from their right, under which our ranks were broken and became massed together as we endeavored to change front to the left to meet them. The immediate attack on our front was destroyed by our first fire. The officers made every possible effort to form their men, and Captains Ashworth and Sterling and Lieutenants Ruth and Funk were all wounded. The regiment, broken and scattered, retreated to the wood around the hospital and maintained a scattering fire. Here, with the broken remnants of other regiments, they defended the fence of the hospital grounds with great determination. Finding the enemy were moving out on our left flank, with the intention of closing in on the only opening into the barricade, I reported the fact to the division commander, and by his directions returned to the fence barricade. The rebels, advancing on our left flank, soon turned the position, and our regimental colors, with the few men left with them, moved out of the hospital grounds through the town to our present position, where we now have almost exactly one-fourth of our force and one commissioned officer besides myself.

I beg particularly to call attention to the meritorious conduct of Sergeant [William] Hardy, color-bearer, who carried off the regimental colors, the staff shot to pieces in his hands; also to the gallantry of Captain Ashworth and Lieutenant Ruth, both wounded; also to Lieutenants Funk and Dorr and Captain Sterling. Acting Sergeant-Major [Henry M.] Copland, Sergeant [Henry H.] Herpst, in command of Company A, and Sergeant [Charles] Winkworth are all deserving of high commendation; also Corporal [John M.] Bingham, of Company A. The constant changes of position which the regiment was ordered to make, and the seeming uncertainty of which way we were to expect an attack, or what position we were to defend, was exceedingly trying to the discipline of the regiment. Their conduct was, in my opinion, far beyond praise. I also wish to call attention to those whom the men speak of as deserving of high commendation—Sergeants Robert [F.] Bates, [William A.] McCoy, [Joshua L.] Childs (wounded, who insisted on remaining with his company), [John] McTaggart, James Allen, and Charles Barlow, Corporals Daniel H. Weikel and [Edward D.] Knight, and Privates T. B. H. McPherson and William Branson.

UNIT: 142nd Infantry. **OTHER NAME:** None.

ORGANIZATION: I Corps, 3rd Div., 1st Brig.

ORGANIZED: From the counties of Fayette, Luzerne, Mercer, Monroe, Somerset, Venango, & Westmoreland. **MUSTERED:** Camp Curtin, Harrisburg, Aug., 1st, 1862.

COMMANDER: 1) Col. Robert P. Cummings (1827-1863), mortally wounded on July 1st, died on July 2nd. 2) Lt. Col. Alfred B. McCalmont (1825-1874), assumed command.

MONUMENT LOCATION: On Reynolds Ave., a few yards south of its intersection with Meridith Ave., southeast of the Herbst Woods on the east crest of McPherson Ridge. Monument is for reference only. The regiment was in several positions facing different directions at different times. **Map:** I, E-3.

STRENGTH: 10 Cos, 263 effectives. **LOSSES:** K-12, W-106, M-61. Total: 179. Percent loss: 68.1.

WEAPONS: .58 Springfields.

SUMMARY: Arrived on field with brigade near noon, from the direction of Marsh Creek. Formed line of battle facing due north, at site of present day monument. Wheeled left and advanced in support of Cooper's Battery B, First Pennsylvania Light Artillery. Went into second position facing due west, toward and above Willoughby Run, 300 yards west of present day monument. Advanced into Run with brigade, meeting heavy infantry and artillery fire. Withdrew east of the Run, going back into position on

Cooper's right rear at the site of the monument on S. Reynolds Ave. Took heavy casualties from enemy artillery fire intended for Cooper's battery. Retired with Cooper into the swale between McPherson and Seminary ridges. Pressed back grudgingly to the woodlot just west of the Lutheran Theological Seminary. Swept off Seminary Ridge fighting to the last, losing many wounded and killed after fresh Confederate reinforcements overwhelmed them. Retreated sem-organized through the southern edge of town. Reformed on south Cemetery Hill.

Report of Lieut. Col. Alfred B. McCalmont, One hundred and forty-second Pennsylvania Infantry. NEAR GETTYSBURG, PA., July 4, 1863.
SIR: On the night of the 1st, the men under my command, numbering 80 for duty, lay on their arms in the rear of batteries at the cemetery, and under orders to support them in the event of an attack.

UNIT: 151st Infantry. **OTHER NAME:** None.

ORGANIZATION: I Corps, 3rd Div., 1st Brig.

ORGANIZED: From the counties of Berks, Juniata, Pike, Susquehanna, & Warren. **MUSTERED:** Camp Curtin, Harrisburg, Oct. 1862. Nine month regiment whose enlistment was nearly up.

COMMANDER: 1) Lt. Col. George F. McFarland (1834-1891), wounded in action on July 1st. 2) Capt. Walter L. Owens (1840-1912), assumed command.

MONUMENT LOCATION: In Herbst Woods on East McPherson Ridge, just a few yards northwest of the intersection of Meridith & Reynolds Avenues. Monument doesn't reflect the western most advanced position. **Map:** I, E-3.

STRENGTH: 10 Cos, 467 effectives. **LOSSES:** K-51, W-211, M-75, Total: 337. Percent Loss: 72.2.

At Gettysburg

WEAPONS: .577 Enfields.

SUMMARY: Advanced into line of battle near noon in support of the Iron Brigade. Moved into the open meadow south of the Herbst Woods, near present monument, the right flank a few yards into the woods itself. Continued to the west-northwest moving deeper into the woods. Skirmishers actively engaged with enemy. Advanced to Willoughby Run with brigade, repulsed with light losses. Reorganized in rear of the Iron Brigade, along Reynolds Ave. Stubbornly held its ground throughout the afternoon. Withdrew toward Seminary Ridge into the woodlot just west of the main Lutheran Seminary building in support of Cooper's Pennsylvania battery. Again held its ground, taking heavy casualties. Forced back to Seminary Ridge, broken up when flanked and pressed. Survivors formed a defensive line with other I Corps troops as the artillery near the main building was allowed to pull out, without losing a gun. Retreated through town to South Cemetery Hill.

Ranks first of all Federal regiments at Gettysburg in total wounded, (211 vs. 24th Mich., 210), second in total aggregate casualties (24 Mich. 363 vs. 337), fifth in total killed and ninth in total percentage lost. The small numbers captured, compared with the total wounded, reflect the determination of the men from the 151st. The highest casualty rate sustained by a Confederate regiment was the 26th North Carolina, which attacked these two Federal regiments in this area.

Report of Lieut. Col. George F. McFarland, One hundred and fifty-first Pennsylvania Infantry. March 15, 1864.
General: Our arrival at this point was greeted by the booming of cannon, Buford's cavalry, dismounted, with some artillery having engaged the enemy—the advance of Pender's division of A. P. Hill's corps—a short time previous. Without delay the brigade advanced obliquely to the right, over a small open hollow, to the edge of a ridge west of the Theological Seminary. Here, by the order of General Rowley, knapsacks were unslung, after which we advanced to the top of the ridge. About the same time, General Reynolds having been killed, General Doubleday, our division commander, took command of the corps, General Rowley of the division, and Colonel Biddle, of the One hundred and twenty-first

Regiment Pennsylvania Volunteers, of the brigade.

All firing now ceased for perhaps an hour, when, about noon, the enemy opened on our right. As this was a flank fire, we were soon ordered back into the hollow. Here, guarding the batteries, we were subject to a constant fire of shot and shell for two hours and a half, frequently changing our position. About 2 p.m. the One hundred and fifty-first Pennsylvania Volunteers was detached from the brigade by General Rowley, and ordered to take a position behind a fence running along the south end of the seminary grove.

By this time a line of battle was forming in our front, which soon after advanced to the ridge west of the seminary, occupied earlier in the day. In this line there was a gap or interval left immediately in our front between the balance of our own brigade and General Meredith's brigade, of the First Division, on the right. Into this interval the One hundred and fifty-first Pennsylvania Volunteers was ordered by General Rowley in person, and, crossing the breastwork behind which it lay, it advanced and closed the interval. The position of the regiment was now such that a little more than one-half of its left wing extended beyond the strip of woods on the ridge directly west of the seminary. The enemy greeted me with a volley which brought several of my men down, where I had halted in position. Having previously cautioned the men against excitement and firing at random, and the enemy being partly concealed in the woods on lower ground than we occupied, I did not order them to fire a regular volley, but each man to fire as he saw an enemy on which to take a steady aim. This was strictly observed, and during the next hour's terrific fighting many of the enemy were brought low.

I know not how men could have fought more desperately, exhibited more coolness, or contested the field with more determined courage than did those of the One hundred and fifty-first Pennsylvania Volunteers on that ever-memorable day. But the fire of the enemy, at least two to one, was very severe and destructive, and my gallant officers and men fell thick and fast. This was especially true after he, while moving to outflank the forces on my left, suffered very heavily from our deliberate oblique fire; for exasperated, no doubt, by this, his fire was now concentrated upon us. Notwithstanding this, the regiment held its ground and maintained the unequal contest until the forces both on my right and left had fallen back and gained a considerable distance to the rear. Then, finding that I was entirely unsupported, exposed to a rapidly increasing fire in front, and in danger of being surrounded, I ordered the regiment to fall back, which it did in good order, to the temporary breastwork from which it had advanced, the enemy following closely, but cautiously. Here I halted, with fragments of Meredith's brigade on my right and portions of the Twentieth New York State Militia, One hundred and twenty-first Pennsylvania Volunteers, and One hundred and forty second Pennsylvania Volunteers, on my left. An unknown mounted officer brought me the flag of this latter regiment to know whether it was mine. The colonel having already fallen, I ordered it to be placed on my left, and portions of the regiment rallied around it and fought bravely.

We now quickly checked the advance of the enemy. In fact, having the advantage of breastworks and woods, our fire was so destructive that the enemy's lines in front were broken, and his first attempt to flank us greeted with such an accurate oblique fire that it failed. But in a second attempt, made soon after, he gained our left flank, moving in single file and at double-quick. Up to this time the officers and men under my command had fought with the determined courage of veterans, and an effectiveness which the enemy himself respected and afterward acknowledged (to me in conversation while a prisoner in their hands). Not a man had left the ranks, even to carry a wounded comrade to the rear. But the regiment had lost terribly, and now did not number one-fourth of what it did two hours earlier in the day. The enemy, on the contrary, had increased, and was now rapidly forming on my left. All support had left both flanks and were already well to the rear. Hence I ordered the shattered remnants of as brave a regiment as ever entered the field to fall back, and accompanied it a few paces. Then stopping, perhaps 20 paces from the seminary, I turned, and, stooping down, examined the condition of the enemy in front.

At that instant, 4. 20 p. m., I was hit by a flank fire in both legs at the same instant, which caused the amputation of my right leg, and so shattered my left that it is now, at the end of eight and a half months, still unhealed and unserviceable. I was carried into the seminary by Private [Lyman D.] Wilson, of Company F, the only man near me, and who narrowly escaped, a ball carrying away the middle button on my coat-sleeve while my arm was around his neck.

The regiment, passing on, had gained the north end of the seminary, and was fortunately covered from the flank fire (volley) which wounded me. It moved through the town to Cemetery Hill, where 8 officers and 113 men answered to roll-call next morning, though 21 officers and 446 men had gone into the fight. Two captains remained, one of whom (Captain Owens, of Company D) commanded the regiment during the second and third days of the battle. . . . It is with pleasure that I refer to the bravery and efficiency of the officers and the heroic, self-sacrificing spirit manifested by the men of the One hundred and fifty-first Pennsylvania Volunteers.

I regret the loss of the many gallant patriots who lost their lives or received honorable scars in its ranks; but I rejoice it was in the battle of Gettysburg and in defense of human freedom and republican institutions.

UNIT: 1st Pennsylvania Light Artillery, Battery B. **OTHER NAME:** "43rd Volunteers," "Cooper's battery".

ORGANIZATION: I Corps Artillery Brigade.

ORGANIZED: From the county of Lawrence. **MUSTERED:** Mount Jackson, Aug. 5, 1861.

COMMANDER: Capt. James H. Cooper (1840-1906).

MONUMENT LOCATION: On Reynolds Ave., 2/3 of a mile north of Fairfield Rd. on the crest of East McPherson Ridge. The monument is for reference only as the unit had three different positions. **Map:** I, E-3.

STRENGTH: 106 effectives (many volunteer infantrymen). **LOSSES:** K-3, W-9, M-0. Total: 12. Percent Loss: 11.3.

WEAPONS: Four 3-inch Ordnance Rifles.

At Gettysburg

SUMMARY: Arrived from the direction of Marsh Creek, going into battery in an oat field on the western brow of McPherson's Ridge, several hundred yards west of the present-day monument. Opened on surprised enemy artillery with telling effect, forcing one battery off Herr Ridge. As ordered, Cooper turned his attention to Confederate infantry west of Willoughby Run, in a vain attempt to cover a futile attack by a Federal brigade to dislodge the enemy. The Confederate battery Cooper had driven off reappeared only 700 yards away at right enfilade and opened on Battery B, forcing Cooper back to where the monument is now located. Spent the last hour on McPherson Ridge near present day marker in both counter-infantry and artillery fire.

As ordered, pulled back into the swale east of McPherson's Ridge, faced north and engaged against infantry and artillery fire. Pressed from the west, Cooper, as ordered, pulled back to the woodlot on Seminary Ridge and engaged at close quarters with three guns, one having been disabled. Retired to the north of the main seminary building and re-opened again. Successfully pulled out with the enemy among the guns. Retreated through town to East Cemetery Hill.

Report of Capt. James H. Cooper, Battery B, First Pennsylvania Light Artillery. Hdqrs. Battery B, First Pa. Art., July 17, 1863.

Adjutant: On the morning of the 1st of July, the battery marched from camp near Emmitsburg, Md., to the vicinity of Gettysburg, Pa. where it was placed in position by Colonel Wainwright, about 12 m., on the left of the Third Division, First Army Corps, and fired about twenty-five shots at a battery in front, which was firing upon the infantry of the corps and Captain Hall's battery. This battery soon ceased firing, and another directly on the right opened, when we changed front to the right, by order of Colonel Wainwright, and engaged it for a few minutes, when the colonel ordered the battery to be placed in position near the Gettysburg Seminary. Here it remained unengaged for a few minutes, when a battery in front again opened and fired a few minutes, when the enemy's infantry made its appearance along the woods and crest in our front. The fire of the battery was then concentrated upon them, case shot and shell being used until canister range was obtained, and this, with the assistance of Lieutenant Stewart's and Captain Stevens' batteries, reduced the enemy's lines very much. At about 5 p. m., all infantry support having been driven back, the battery was compelled to retire through Gettysburg to Cemetery Hill.

In this day's engagement about 400 rounds of ammunition were expended, but three guns being engaged, one axle having broken from recoil at the first few shots. The following are the casualties of this day's engagement, viz: Lieutenant Miller, wounded slightly; Private A. P. Alcorn, wounded severely and taken prisoner; Private John Pauly, wounded severely; Private John W. Phillips, wounded severely; Private Asahel Shaffer, wounded slightly; 2 horses killed.

UNIT: 149th Infantry (Co. D detached) **OTHER NAME:** "Second (Bogus) Bucktails".

ORGANIZATION: I Corps, 3rd Div., 2nd Brig.

ORGANIZED: From the counties of Clearfield, Huntingdon, Lebanon, Mifflin, Potter, and Tioga. **MUSTERED:** Camp McNeil, Harrisburg, Aug. 30, 1862.

COMMANDER: 1) Col. Walton Dwight (1837-1878), wounded in action on July 1st. 2) Capt. James Glenn (1824-1901), assumed command.

MONUMENT LOCATION: At the intersection of Reynolds Ave., and Chambersburg Pike on the crest of West McPherson Ridge. Monument is located at the exact position the regiment held for most of the day's battle. **Map:** I, G-3.

STRENGTH: 9 Cos, 450 effectives. **LOSSES:** K-53, W-172, M-111. Total: 336. Percent Loss: 74.7.

WEAPONS: .577 Enfields.

SUMMARY: Moved onto West McPherson Ridge and into

line of battle, facing both west and north, at the intersection of the Chambersburg Pike and the McPherson farm lane, presently Stone Ave. Due to accurate Confederate artillery fire the regimental colors were moved north across the pike, and into a wheatfield to draw enemy fire away from the men while they laid south of the pike. Charged the Railroad Cut twice, taking huge losses. Nearly cut off by Daniels' North Carolina Brigade from the north, and Brockenbrough's Virginians from the south and west, the 149th fought its way back from the Rail Road Cut taking many casualties. Friendly artillery fire brought down many retreating men. Retreated disorganized back to Seminary Ridge where the survivors made several stands with other fugitives. Retreated through town to south Cemetery Hill. Ranks third of all Federal regiments in total combined losses, fourth in total number killed, sixth in total number wounded, and seventh in highest casualty percentages and men missing.

Report of Col. Roy Stone, One Hundred and forty-ninth Pennsylvania Infantry and commanding Second Brigade. ,— —, 1863.

GENERAL: I have the honor to report that, in accordance with orders received directly from yourself, at 11 o'clock a. m., July 1, I posted my brigade (One hundred and forty-third, One hundred and forty-ninth, and One hundred and fiftieth Pennsylvania Volunteers) between the two brigades of Wadsworth's division, upon the ridge in advance of Seminary Ridge, my right resting upon the Chambersburg or Cashtown road and left extending nearly to the wood occupied by General Meredith's brigade, with a strong force of skirmishers thrown well down the next slope, and the road held by a platoon of sharpshooters. The skirmishers having to advance over an open field, without the slightest shelter, and under a hot fire from the enemy's skirmishers concealed behind a fence, did not stop to fire a shot, but, dashing forward at a full run, drove the rebel line from the fence, and held it throughout the day. As we came upon the field, the enemy opened fire upon us from two batteries on the opposite ridge, and continued it, with some intermissions, during the action. Our low ridge afforded slight shelter from this fire, but no better was attainable, and our first disposition was unchanged until between 12 and 1 o'clock, when a new battery upon a hill on the extreme right opened a most destructive enfilade of our line, and at the same time all the troops upon my right fell back nearly a half mile to the Seminary Ridge. This made my position hazardous and difficult in the extreme, but rendered its maintenance all the more important. I threw one regiment (One hundred and forty-ninth, Lieutenant-Colonel Dwight commanding) into the road, and disposed the others on the left of the stone building, to conceal them from the enfilading battery. My line thus formed a right angle facing north and west. . . . At about 1:30 p. m. the grand advance of the enemy's infantry began. From my position I was enabled to trace their formation for at least 2 miles. It appeared to be a nearly continuous line of deployed battalions, with other battalions in mass or reserve. Their line being formed not parallel but obliquely to ours, their left first became engaged with the troops on the northern prolongation of Seminary Ridge. The battalions engaged soon took a direction parallel to those opposed to them, thus causing a break in their line and exposing the flank of those engaged to the fire of my two regiments in the Chambersburg road. Though at the longest range of our pieces, we poured a most destructive fire upon their flanks, and, together with the fire in their front, scattered them over the fields.

A heavy force was then formed in two lines parallel to the Chambersburg road, and pressed forward to the attack of my position. Anticipating this, I had sent Colonel Dwight (One hundred and forty-ninth) forward to occupy a deep railroad cutting about 100 yards from the road, and when they came to a fence within pistol-shot of his line he gave them a staggering volley; reloading as they climbed the fence, and waiting till they came within 30 yards, gave them another volley, and charged, driving them back over the fence in utter confusion.

Returning to the cut, he found that the enemy had planted a battery which perfectly enfiladed and made it untenable, and he was obliged to fall back to the road.

No language can do justice to the conduct of my officers and men on the bloody "first day;" to the coolness with which they watched and awaited, under a fierce storm of shot and shell, the approach of the enemy's overwhelming masses; their ready obedience to orders, and the prompt and perfect execution, under fire, of all the tactics of the battle-field; to the fierceness of their repeated attacks, or to the desperate tenacity of their resistance.

They fought as if each man felt that upon his own arm hung the fate of the day and the nation. Nearly two-thirds of my command fell on the field. Every field officer save one was wounded and disabled. Not one of them left the field until completely disabled.

UNIT: 150th Infantry (Co D detached as Lincoln's personal guard). **OTHER NAME:** "Third (Bogus) Bucktails."

ORGANIZATION: I Corps, 3rd Div., 2nd Brig.

ORGANIZED: From the counties of Crawford, McKean, Philadelphia, & Union. **MUSTERED:** Camp Curtin, Harrisburg, Sept. 4th, 1862.

COMMANDER: 1) Col. Langhorne Wister (1834-1891), assumed command of brigade on field of battle on July 1st. Wounded during same engagement. 2) Lt. Col. Henry Huidkoper (1839-1918), assumed command of regiment on Wister's promotion, wounded in action on July 1st. 3) Capt. George W. Jones (1833-1913), assumed command upon Huidkoper's wounding. Huidkoper received the Medal of Honor for his service on July 1st.

MONUMENT LOCATION: Located on the Edward McPherson farm, West McPherson Ridge, along Stone Ave., 100 yards south of its intersection with Chambersburg Pike. Stone Ave. was at the time of the battle the McPherson Farm lane. **Map:** I, G-3.

STRENGTH: 9 Cos, 400 effectives. **LOSSES:** K-35, W-152, M-77. Total: 264. Percent Loss: 66.0.

WEAPONS: .58 Springfields & .577 Enfields.

SUMMARY: Arrived on West McPherson Ridge and took position on the left of the brigade, occupying the McPherson farm, from the house south toward the Herbst Woods. Five companies detached from the right of the regiment, while the left four formed a single line in the farm lane facing west, near present monument on Stone Ave., and sent north to help the 149th & 143rd at the railroad cut. Pulled back to the McPherson farm after the successful charge. Holding onto the McPherson farm, the 150th withdrew only after being flanked on the right rear from the north.

A stone quarry to the front of the 150th forced attacking Virginians from Brockenbrough's brigade to detour to the south and charge around the obstruction. This formed a funnel which grouped Brockenbrough's lines into a mass when they crested the ridge between the quarry's right wall and the Herbst Woods, a 200-yard gap. Four desperate attempts were made to take the farm, all failed. The Virginians, mingled with a North Carolina regiment farther south, were they able to flank the 150th from the Herbst Woods and carry the ridge. Survivors reunited on Seminary Ridge for one last stand before being forced back through town to South Cemetery Hill.

Report of Lieut. Col. Henry S. Huidekoper, One hundred and fiftieth Pennsylvania Infantry. —, —, 63.

SIR: About noon arrived on the battle-field at Gettysburg. Rapidly throwing off their knapsacks, the regiment moved up on the ground between the Iron Brigade and the other regiments of Colonel Stone's brigade, which reached to the Chambersburg road. After lying under shelling for an hour, the command of the regiment fell to me, Colonel Wister taking command of the brigade. Almost immediately, by order of Colonel Wister, a change of front forward on first company was made with regularity and promptness, and in that new position, protected by a fence, our men awaited the charge of a rebel regiment . . . At the distance of 50 yards, a volley was poured into the rebels, which staggered them so completely that a second one was fired before an attempt was made to advance or retreat. At this juncture, Colonel Wister ordered the regiment to charge, and led it in person. The rebels were utterly routed, and the colors of the One hundred and forty-ninth Pennsylvania Volunteers, which had been lost, were recaptured and restored to that regiment.

The One hundred and fiftieth then fell back to the position from which it had advanced. The firing of the enemy, who was approaching in front of the corps, now became fearful, and the regiment changed front to rear to meet this new attack. The movement was made in perfect order, and then bravely did the men move to the front, following the color-sergeant, who rushed to place his standard on the small rise of ground in advance. Four companies again changed front to resist the flank attack, while the remainder of the regiment fought one entire brigade, which was prevented from advancing by a high fence. The severe loss attending fighting at such odds soon compelled our men to give way, but a battery coming up on our left, another stand was necessary, and again was the regiment moved forward until the battery had wheeled around and moved to the rear. At this moment a wound compelled me to relinquish the command to Captain Widdis, Major Chamberlain having been severely wounded some time before.

I cannot praise too highly the conduct of both officers and men. It was all that could have been desired. Among the many brave, I would especially commend for coolness and courage Major Chamberlain, Adjutant Ashurst, Lieutenants Sears, Chancellor (who lost his leg and has since died), Bell, Kilgore, Color-bearer [John] Pieffer. Sergeant [Duffy B.] Torbett, and Corporal [Roe] Reisinger. The regiment numbered, including 17 officers, before the battle nearly 400 at roll-call; in the evening but 2 officers, 1 of those wounded, and 84 men were present.

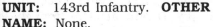

UNIT: 143rd Infantry. **OTHER NAME:** None.

ORGANIZATION: I Corps, 3rd Div., 2nd Brig.

ORGANIZED: From the counties of Luzerne and Susquehanna. **Mustered:** Camp Luzerne, Wilkes Barre, Sept. 1, 1862.

COMMANDER: 1) Col. Edmond L. Dana (1817-1889), assumed command of brigade. 2) Lt. Col. John D. Musser (1826-1864), assumed command of regiment on Dana's field promotion.

MONUMENT LOCATION: On the east crest of McPherson Ridge at Reynolds Ave.& Chambersburg Pike. The monument represents the regiment's first position. **Map:** I, G-3.

STRENGTH: 10 Cos, 465 effectives. **LOSSES:** K-21, W-141, M-91. Total: 253. Percent Loss: 54.4.

WEAPONS: .58 Springfields & .577 Enfields.

SUMMARY: Arrived on the Chambersburg Pike near present monument facing due north, taking heavy casualties from enfilading artillery fire from Herr Ridge. Attempted to support artillery battery in an untenable position on top of east crest of McPherson's Ridge. This position was shortlived as the regiment changed direction to the west by moving into the McPherson farmyard to meet threat from Willoughby Run. A stone quarry below the west brow of McPherson's Ridge, and east of Willoughby Run, gave the regiment a much-needed rest as a direct frontal assault from Herr Ridge on their position was impossible.

Pulled back to their original position along the Chambersburg Pike, near present monument, advanced in a counter-charge on the railroad grading, driving Daniels' North Carolina Brigade back. Out flanked on the right by a second charge by Daniels, and flanked on the left and rear, the 143rd withdrew, leaving many wounded and dead. Caught in a semi circle of advancing enemy, they were fired on by friendly artillery from the eastern railroad cut and along the Chambersburg Pike posted on top of Seminary Ridge. The regiment broke to the rear in a slow unorganized retreat. Rallied on Seminary Ridge, retreated through town to Cemetery Hill.

Report of Lieut. Col. John D. Musser, One hundred and forty-third Pennsylvania Infantry. Camp near Gettysburg, July 4, 1863.
Colonel: . . . after the command was turned over to me, which occurred while holding the road west of the town, where the One hundred and forty-ninth and One hundred and forty-third had been ordered by command of Colonel Stone. It was in the hottest of the fire that I assumed the command, and had simply to hold the position, which we did as long as it could be held without being all captured, as the

enemy were rapidly falling back on our left and flanking us on the right. Up to this time but few had been killed or wounded. Capts. G. N. Reichard, Plotz, and Conyngham, among the officers, were wounded early in the action; Captain Reichard alone left on the field. After the enemy had driven the One hundred and forty-ninth from our left, I gave the command to move back. After crossing the crest of a hill, which lay a quarter of a mile in our rear and toward the town, we halted, faced about, and fired several volleys, checking their advance in front but not on our flanks. We then fell back to a peach orchard, where our battery was stationed. We again halted, and, with others, saved the battery, leaving the men (not ours) to pull it out of range by hand. It was with great difficulty I could get all the men to fall back from this point, which was a good one, and in front of which the enemy fell thick and fast. Still they moved in columns on our right and left, and superior numbers compelled us to fall back to the town, which, I might say, was done in good order, and only when peremptorily ordered to do so. The road from this hill (Battery Hill) to town was 10 to 12 feet high, and crossed over a stream and low meadow. Before leaving, the enemy had come out of the woods on our right (as we faced the enemy at the battery), and it was while going through the meadow my men fell so rapidly that I concluded to take them on the other side of this high road. But the balls and shell were as thick, if not thicker, on the right as on the left side. While making the observation, I received a ball through my pants, slightly wounding the skin near the knee. I rejoined the regiment, knowing this to be the safest side. I felt like making another stand, but utter destruction would have been inevitable, as the enemy deployed as soon as they left the woods, making intervals between their men, which gave them a decided advantage over us. I am pleased to say my men behaved nobly, and fought under great disadvantage and against greatly superior numbers. Among the officers killed I have to record that of Lieut. Charles W. Betzenberger, who was wounded in the hand early in the action, but nobly stood at the head of his company while supporting the battery in the peach orchard. He moved back only when ordered, and fell, mortally wounded, near the town. Among the wounded I have the honor to report the name of Capt. Charles M. Conyngham, of Company A, who was wounded while out skirmishing, but remained with his company, and remained at the peach orchard until the order was given to move back. I saw him, after we had passed through the town, seemingly exhausted, and ordered my horse back to help him up the hill, but, just as he was mounting, he was again shot in the hip, after which I did not see him, but am happy to report his wounds are not of a dangerous character. Lieut. C. C. Plotz was wounded early in the action, and also afterward again on the road into town. Capt. George N. Reichard, of Company C, was wounded in the shoulder while holding the road, and afterward taken prisoner. Capt. Asher Gaylord, of Company D, was wounded in both legs while in the peach orchard, and left on the field. Lieut. William Lafrance, of Company E, was shot through the arm while passing through the town. Capt. William A. Tubbs, slight wound in head and taken prisoner. Lieut. H. M. Gordon, shot through the leg, and taken prisoner while crawling after the regiment. Lieut. Lyman R. Nicholson, wounded through the shoulder after leaving the peach orchard; supposed to be of a serious character, but refused to have any one remain with him on the field. Lieut. O. E. Vaughan, of Company K, received a slight bruise on the head from a ball, although not close enough to cut the skin, yet may properly be called a wound. I am happy to say that among those not killed or wounded, all, with one exception, stood at their posts and acted in the most becoming and commendable manner, deserving of the highest praise and commendation. John Jones, Jr., adjutant, reported himself wounded, although I have not been able to learn where, or whether sufficiently serious to have prevented him rejoining his regiment after passing through the town, and therefore report him among the doubtful. Lieut. Benjamin F. Walters, of the One hundred and forty-third Regiment, but on your staff, showed great bravery, and distinguished himself, being conspicuous on all parts of the field; but I suppose he will come more properly under the head of your report.

UNIT: 11th Infantry. **OTHER NAME:** None.

ORGANIZATION: I Corps, 2nd Div., 2nd Brig

ORGANIZED: From the Counties of Allegheny, Carbon, Clinton, Cumberland, Lycoming, and Westmorland.
MUSTERED: Camp Curtin, Harrisburg, Nov. 10, 1861.

At Gettysburg

COMMANDER: 1) Col. Richard Coulter (1827-1908), promoted to brigade command on field of battle, July 1st. 2) Capt. Benjamin F. Haines (1835-1903), wounded in action on July 1st. 3) Capt. John B. Overmyer (1842-1903), assumed command.

MONUMENT LOCATION: Atop east Oak Ridge on Doubleday Ave. representing the second position occupied by the regiment, the first being 200 yards to the rear, and below, along the Mummasburg Road facing due north. **Map:** I, C-6.

STRENGTH: 10 Cos, 270 effectives. **LOSSES:** K-1, W-66, M-60, Total: 127. Percentage loss: 47.

WEAPONS: .69 rifled Springfields.

SUMMARY: Faced north along the Mummasburg Road, southeast of monument and below the crest, holding the extreme right of Baxter's brigade. Helped in the repulse of O'Neal's Alabama Brigade which attacked from the McLean farm, located 1/4 mile north of the Mummasburg Road. After O'Neal's repulse, the regiment filed to the southwest, staying below the crest of east Oak Ridge. On orders the 11th stood and fired into Iverson's North Carolina Brigade as it attacked obliquely from the northwest. Crossed over the stone wall east of the monument and counter-charged Iverson's brigade taking many prisoners. On its withdrawal off Oak Ridge, several companies stopped and helped cover the withdrawal of Stewart's 4th U. S. Battery B from the eastern railroad cut. Retreated through town to Cemetery Hill. July 2nd & 3rd. Moved to various parts of the field on Cemetery Hill and Ridge in support of batteries. Did not engage. Held their position in reserve from July 3rd to July 5th in Zeigler's Grove. Detailed to bury dead and collect arms.

Report of Col. Richard Coulter, Eleventh Pennsylvania Infantry, commanding regiment and First Brigade. GETTYS-

BURG, PA., July 6, 1863

SIR: The First Division had been for some time engaged when this brigade, about 11 a. m., was massed on the west side and near the embankment of the railroad. At this point I was directed by the general commanding the brigade to proceed with the Ninety-seventh New York Volunteers, Colonel Wheelock, and my own, Eleventh Regiment Pennsylvania Volunteers, which I did, deploying both regiments, and moved with skirmishers about a quarter of a mile beyond the railroad track. Discovering that the enemy's movement was being directed against the left flank, I changed front to the left and took position on the ridge (where the fighting subsequently took place), connecting the left of my command upon the right of Gen. Cutler's brigade, of the First Division. I was here joined on the right by General Baxter, who resumed command of the entire line.

The skirmishers had been a short time engaged, and about 1 p. m. the firing became general along the entire line. The enemy after several attempts, finding it impossible to force our position, commenced moving his troops toward the left, under a galling and effective fire from our line. While this was being done, a sally was made by part of the brigade (the Ninety-seventh New York Volunteers and my own regiment engaging in it), which resulted in the capture of about 500 of the enemy.

The line was steadily maintained under a brisk fire until after 3 p. m., at which time, the ammunition being exhausted, we were relieved by a portion of the First Brigade. Upon being so relieved, the regiment was moved to the railroad embankment on the left, and there remained in support of a battery until ordered to fall back the town of Gettysburg, the enemy having in the meantime turned both flanks; then retired with the brigade along the railroad, suffering most severely from a galling fire of musketry and artillery. The division immediately assumed another position in the rear of the town on Cemetery Hill. Here my regiment was transferred to the First Brigade and I assumed the command of the brigade.

UNIT: 88th Infantry. **OTHER NAME:** "Cameron Light Guards."

At Gettysburg

ORGANIZATION: I Corps, 2nd Div., 2nd Brig.

ORGANIZED: From the counties of Berks & Philadelphia. **MUSTERED:** Camp Stokey, Philadelphia, Pennsylvania, Sept. 13, 1861.

COMMANDER: 1) Maj. Benezet F. Foust (1840-1870), wounded in action on July 1st. 2) Capt. Edmond A. Mass (1834-1894), captured on July 1st. 3) Capt. Henry Whiteside (1835-1905), assumed command.

MONUMENT LOCATION: 1) On the west side of Doubleday Ave., 100 yards south of the Mummasburg Rd. on the crest of east Oak Ridge. Monument represents the second position occupied by regiment. 2) Located in the field about 50 yards southwest of above monument. This monument represents the regiment's farthest position west, after charging Iverson's North Carolina Brigade and capturing three regimental flags. **Map:** I, B-5/6.

STRENGTH: 10 Cos, 274 effectives. **LOSSES:** K-4, W- 55, M-51. Total: 110. Percent Loss: 40.1.

WEAPONS: .58 Springfields, .577 Enfields & .69 smoothbores.

SUMMARY: Arrived on field with the brigade and took position along the Mummasburg Road facing due north, second regiment from the left, about 200 yards east and below present monument. Charged O'Neal's Alabama Brigade striking its right flank, which was in the air. Captured one battle flag. Withdrew back to first position, filed to the west, in rear of the 90th Pennsylvania regiment and went into line of battle below the crest of east Oak Ridge, facing due west. Stood and delivered crippling volley into the left flank of Iverson. Charged over the stone wall along present Doubleday Ave., capturing many prisoners and another regimental color. Retreated southeast off ridge with brigade via the railroad grading, through town and on to Cemetery Hill.

Reorganized and was sent into Zeiglers' Grove, located on Cemetery Ridge west of and below Cemetery Hill.

Report of Capt. Edmund Y. Patterson, Eighty-eighth Pennsylvania Infantry. August 22, 1863.
[July 1] About 11 a. m., while marching along, we heard cannonading, and after marching in quick and double-quick time some 2 miles, we were drawn up in line of battle along a stone fence. We then changed our position by left flank, file left, which brought us on a slight hill, and we immediately engaged the enemy, who were advancing on us. Having expended nearly all our ammunition, we charged upon the enemy, capturing a number of prisoners and the colors of the Twenty-third North Carolina and Sixteenth Alabama Regiments. Returning to the line of battle, we continued to fire the few remaining cartridges on hand until we found that the enemy were flanking us, when we fell back through the town, the enemy rapidly following and firing upon us. A new line of battle was formed and cartridges distributed. We then took a position on the left of the hill, which was afterward the center of the line of battle, and threw up breastworks made of rails and earth.

UNIT: 90th Infantry. **OTHER NAME:** None.

ORGANIZATION: I Corps, 2nd Div., 2nd Brig.

ORGANIZED: County of Philadelphia. **MUSTERED:** Oxford Park, Philadelphia, Oct. 1, 1861.

COMMANDER: 1) Col. Peter Lyle (1821-1879), assumed command of brigade on field of battle, July 1st. 2) Maj. Alfred J. Sellers (1836-1908), assumed command on Lyle's promotion to brigade commander. Sellers received the Congressional Medal of Honor for his services on July 1st.

MONUMENT LOCATION: On Doubleday Ave., 40 yards southeast of its intersection with the Mummasburg Road just north of the park tower. **Map:** I, B-6.

STRENGTH: 10 Cos, 208 effectives. **LOSSES:** K-8, W-45, M-40. Total: 93. Percent Loss: 44.7.

WEAPONS: .58 Springfields.

SUMMARY: During O'Neal's assault, eight companies faced due north along the Mummasburg Road, while two faced west at the apex of the low stone wall along Doubleday Ave. During Iverson's assault, the eight companies facing north filed to the northwest to align on the right of the two facing west, and counter charged Iverson's left flank, capturing many prisoners. On their withdrawal they retreated through town to Cemetery Hill, moving into Zeigler's Grove before dark.

UNIT: 107th Infantry. **OTHER NAME:** None.

ORGANIZATION: I Corps, 2nd Div., 1st Brig.

ORGANIZED: From the counties of Cumberland, Dauphin, Franklin, Lebanon, and York. **MUSTERED:** Camp Curtin, Harrisburg, Mar. 5, 1861.

COMMANDER: 1) Lt. Col. James M. Thomson (1834-1893), wounded in action on July 1st. 2) Capt. Emanuel D. Roath (1820-1907), assumed command.

MONUMENT LOCATION: On the west shoulder of Doubleday Avenue on the crest of east Oak Ridge. **Map:** I, C-5.

STRENGTH: 10 Cos, 252 effectives. **LOSSES:** K-11, W-56, M- 98. Total: 165. Percent Loss: 64.7.

WEAPONS: .54 Austrian & .577 Enfields.

SUMMARY: Held in reserve on its arrival near the Lutheran Seminary. Led Paul's brigade from the Seminary Ridge north onto east Oak Ridge. Changed from columns of four into line of battle on the double-quick, while obliquing to the northwest and up toward the rockwall on the crest of east Oak Ridge. Went into action on the left of the 11th Pennsylvania at site of present monuments, at precisely the right time. Charged over the rock wall and participated in the destruction of Iverson's Brigade. Held position on the crest to the very last as other regiments melted away during the Confederates' last attacks, giving other units the necessary time needed to withdraw. Took extreme casualties on Oak Ridge as indicated. Retreated disorganized through town after being routed. Reassembled on Cemetery Hill, moved into Zeiglers' Grove at dusk. Ranks fourth in most men captured, and 19th in total percent casualties of all Federal regiments at Gettysburg.

The following is the report of Lieut. Col. J. MacThomson, of the One hundred and seventh Pennsylvania Volunteers, during the action of July 1, at Gettysburg, he being in command up to that time. July 1. —After the engagement, we fell back to the left of Cemetery Hill, and threw up strong breastworks, which we occupied until next morning.

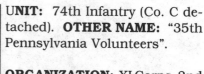

UNIT: 74th Infantry (Co. C detached). **OTHER NAME:** "35th Pennsylvania Volunteers".

ORGANIZATION: XI Corps, 2nd Div., 1st Brig.

ORGANIZED: From the counties of Allegheny and Philadelphia. **MUSTERED:** Camp Wilkens, Pittsburgh, Sept. 14, 1861.

COMMANDER: 1) Col. Adolph Von Hartung (1834-1902), wounded in action on July 1st. 2) Lt. Col. Theobald Von Mitzel (1835-1887). 3) Capt. Henry Krauseneck (1828- ?). Krauseneck was brought up on charges of cowardice for his actions on July 1st & 2nd at Gettysburg. Found guilty in January, 1864, he was allowed to resign his commission from the army.

At Gettysburg

MONUMENT LOCATION: One-quarter mile east of the Mummasburg Road on Howard Ave., the monument represents the regiment's first position. Advanced several hundred yards north past Howard Ave. **Map:** II, D-3.

STRENGTH: 9 Cos, 333 effectives. **LOSSES:** K-10, W-40,

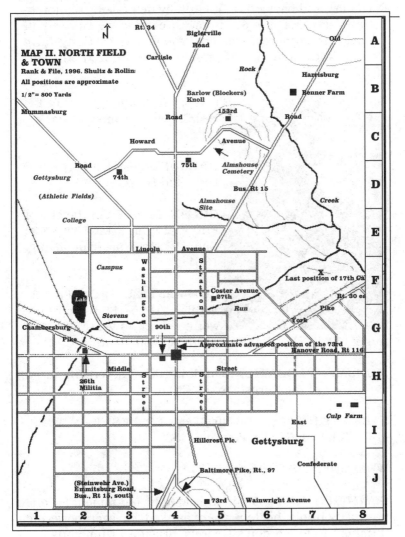

MAP II. NORTH FIELD & TOWN
Rank & File, 1996. Shultz & Rollins
All positions are approximate
1/2" = 800 Yards

M-60. Total: 110. Percent Loss: 33.0.

WEAPONS: .58 Springfield, French, and .577 Enfield.

SUMMARY: Advanced to present day monument in support of Battery L., First Ohio Light Artillery , and laid down in line of battle. Subjected to terrible demoralizing cannon fire from Oak Hill intended for Battery L. Advanced several hundred yards north of the monument, into the fields west of Rock Creek, and engaged Confederates attacking from the McLean farm. Pressed back on right flank by new enemy reinforcements, faced north to meet new threat and were driven off the field in disorder. Retreated through town via Gettysburg College, with many taken prisoner. Reorganized on Cemetery Hill.

UNIT: 75th Infantry. **OTHER NAME:** "40th Pennsylvania Volunteers."

ORGANIZATION: XI Corps, 3rd Div., 2nd Brig.

ORGANIZED: From the city of Philadelphia. **MUSTERED:** Camp Worth, Philadelphia, Aug. 1861.

COMMANDER: 1) Col. Francis Mahler (1826-1863), mortally wounded on July 1st. 2) Maj. August Ledig (1816-1895), assumed command.

MONUMENT LOCATION: On Howard Ave. several hundred yards east of the Carlisle Road. **Map:** II, C-4.

STRENGTH: 9 Cos, 208 effectives. **LOSSES:** K-19, W-89, M-3. Total: 111. Percent Loss: 53.

WEAPONS: .58 Springfields.

SUMMARY: Held position indicated by monument for one hour. Soundly beaten when flanked by over powering numbers from Gordon's Georgia Brigade. Numerous accounts state that the 75th broke before the order was given to withdraw. The low number of men captured (3) may verify that. Retreated in disorder to Cemetery Hill.

At Gettysburg

Report of Maj. August Ledig, Seventy-fifth Pennsylvania Infantry. Hdqrs, Seventy-first Pennsylvania Volunteers, July 28, 1863.

July 1: We were immediately ordered to the north side of the town, where the regiment was placed as follows: On my left (the extreme left of the Second Brigade), the Eighty-second Ohio Volunteers; on my right, the One hundred and nineteenth New York Regiment, in line of battle. Here we received a heavy fire from the enemy's 10-pounder rifled guns, which caused a loss in the regiment of 1 killed and 2 wounded.

About 2 o'clock, the whole brigade advanced nearly one-half mile, which was greatly interrupted by fences, which had to be taken down under a heavy fire of musketry from the enemy. When within 100 yards of them, in a wheat-field, we charged upon them and drove them back. We halted, and opened fire on the enemy. The Eighty-second Ohio, on my left, was flanked, and gave way.

Col. F. Mahler's horse was shot, but he [the colonel] got up again, and went forward to direct the fire to the left flank, which was now unprotected, and the enemy threatening to cut off our retreat. He was already within 40 yards of our left and rear Colonel Mahler at this moment received a severe wound, and was disabled, so I took the command, and directed at once the fire left-oblique, and began to retreat behind a fence, which I could only pass by the flank, moving my left flank through first, so as to give the enemy battle on my left and front.

I began now to retreat about 200 yards into an orchard. The One hundred and nineteenth New York Regiment, on my right, suffered also heavily from the flank attack, and moved backward also in the garden. I received orders to fall back on the town. Here the Second Division arrived and went into the engagement. Shortly after this, a new line behind the town was ordered, and formed by my regiment in the best of order. I was ordered in a corn-field behind a stone wall, below the Evergreen Cemetery, the Eighty-second Ohio on my right, the First Brigade on my left.

On July 2 and 3, the regiment was not actively engaged. I lost here 3 men killed and wounded by the heavy bombardment.

UNIT: 153rd Infantry. **OTHER NAME:** None.

ORGANIZATION: XI Corps, 1st Div., 1st Brig.

ORGANIZED: From the county of Northampton. **MUSTERED:** Camp Curtin, Harrisburg, Oct. 7, 1862. Nine-month regiment whose enlistment was up in eight days. Ninety percent of the survivors of the battle reenlisted for three years.

COMMANDER: Maj. John F. Frueauff (1838-1886).

MONUMENT LOCATION: On East Howard Ave., on the northern crest of Blocker's ("Barlow's") Knoll overlooking Rock Creek. **Map:** II, C-5.

STRENGTH: 10 Cos, 497 effectives. **LOSSES:** K-23, W-142, M-46. Total: 211. Percent Loss: 42.5. **WEAPONS:** .58 Austrians.

SUMMARY: Held position on north brow of Barlow's Knoll above Rock Creek, approximately 75 yards north of monument, with the 68th N.Y. posted below and to its left front. When Gordon's Georgia Brigade attacked in overwhelming numbers the 68th was hit from the front left, left, and left rear, forcing that regiment out of line in panic, and into the left flank of the 153rd. Although strong in numbers, the 153rd's right and center disintegrated as Gordon pressed home his attack, forcing the regiment back up and over Barlow's Knoll, where their monument now stands, while the 68th carried with them most of the 153rd's left flank. Attempted to reorganize south of the knoll near the Alms House Cemetery with another brigade, who itself was under extreme pressure. Faced about on numerous occasions and helped to check Gordon's advance until Confederate reinforcements from the east threatened to cut them off. Retreated in a semi-organized column through town to Cemetery Hill.

UNIT: 27th Infantry (Co F detached) **OTHER NAME:** None.

ORGANIZATION: XI Corps, 2nd Div., 1st Brig.

ORGANIZED: From the county of Philadelphia. **MUSTERED:** Camp Enstein, Camden, New Jersey, May 31, 1861.

COMMANDER: Lt. Col. Lorenz Cantador (1810-1883).

MONUMENT LOCATION: On Coster Ave. 50 yards east of its intersection with Stratton St. Note large mural on wall directly behind the monument depicting the brickyard that once occupied this area, and the regiment's fight. **Map:** II, F-5.

STRENGTH: 9 Cos. 283 effectives. **LOSSES:** K-6, W-29, M-76. Total: 111. Percentage Loss: 39.2.

WEAPONS: .577 Enfields & .69 Smoothbores.

SUMMARY: Held initially in reserve south of town. Advanced with brigade into a brickyard south of Stratton St. Formed line of battle anchoring the brigade's left flank. The 27th stretched from inside the brickyard north to Stratton Street, facing due north. Forced to retire when the two New York regiments on its right were swept away by overpowering numbers from Hay's & Avery's brigades. Most men captured from the 27th were taken inside the brickyard, those north of the gate escaping down Stratton Street. Company A captured one unidentified Confederate battle flag in its rear guard action along Stratton Street during its withdrawal. Reorganized along the Baltimore Pike.

[No monument for July 1. See July 2]
UNIT: 73rd Infantry. **OTHER NAME:** "Pennsylvania Legion, 45th Pennsylvania Volunteers".

ORGANIZATION: XI Corps, 2nd Div., 1st Brig.

ORGANIZED: From the county of Philadelphia. **MUS-TERED:** Lemon Hill, Philadelphia, Sept. 19, 1861.

COMMANDER: Capt. Daniel F. Kelly (1837- ?).

MONUMENT LOCATION: On East Cemetery Hill a few yards east of the Baltimore Pike among the guns of Battery I, First New York Light Artillery. Monument represents their third and final position on July 1st. **Map:** VII, B-3.

STRENGTH: 10 Cos, 290 effectives. **LOSSES:** K-7, W-27, M-0. Total: 34. Percent Loss: 11.7.

WEAPONS: .58 Springfield, .577 Enfield, .54 &. 58 Austrian.

SUMMARY: Advanced with the brigade from a reserve position southeast of town, north toward the fighting. Detached from the brigade, the 73rd continued on its own north up the Baltimore Pike to the diamond in the center of town. Continued north along Carlisle Street in a vain attempt to reach and support Heckman's First Ohio Light Artillery, Battery I. Fleeing Federals made moving forward all but impossible. Returned to diamond, reorganized line, was swept out of town by fleeing mob. Retreated back to Cemetery Hill.

July 2nd

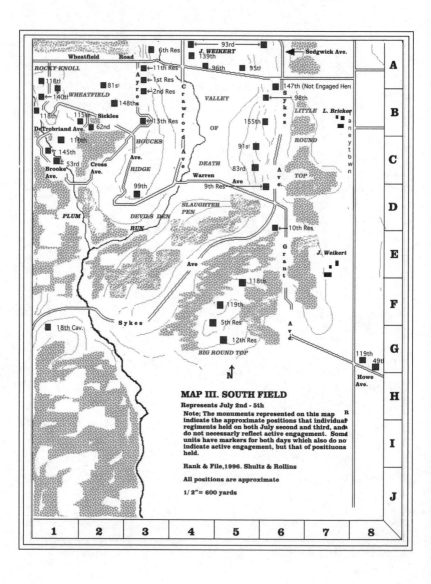

MAP III. SOUTH FIELD

Represents July 2nd - 5th

Note; The monuments represented on this map indicate the approximate positions that individual regiments held on both July second and third, and do not necessarily reflect active engagement. Some units have markers for both days which also do no indicate active engagement, but that of positiuons held.

Rank & File, 1996. Shultz & Rollins

All positions are approximate

1/ 2"= 600 yards

UNIT: 99th Infantry. **OTHER NAME:** None.

ORGANIZATION: III Corps, 1st Div., 2nd Brig.

RAISED: From the counties of Lancaster & Philadelphia. **MUSTERED:** Camp Franklin, Alexandria, Virginia, January, 1862.

COMMANDER: Maj. John W. Moore (1836-1865), KIA at Fort Fisher.

MONUMENT LOCATION: Atop the southern crest of Houck's Ridge, east of Sickles Ave. The monument represents the last position of the regiment before retiring. Moved about prior to this posting. **MAP:** V, G-5.

STRENGTH: 10 Cos, 277 effectives. **LOSSES:** K-18, W-81, M-11, Total: 110. Percent Loss: 39.7

WEAPONS: .54 Austrian.
SUMMARY: First deployed near the western edge of the Rose woods, in rear of the Rose house, advancing when ordered to the Emmitsburg Road to support troops already positioned there. Returned to the northeastern edge of the Rose woods after engaging the enemy as they crossed the Emmitsburg Road, faced southwest anchoring Ward's 2nd Brigade's right flank, approximately 100 yards south of the southeastern corner of the Wheatfield near the intersection of Sickles, Ayres, and Cross Avenues. As ordered, pulled out of line of battle and by columns of four, moved south toward Devil's Den via the Valley of Death below and east of Houck's Ridge. Arrived at the southern end of Houck's Ridge, obliqued to the right (west) and climbed the rocky eastern slope to the crest. Formed line of battle under fire from Benning's Georgia Brigade. The left companies refused (turned) their line at an angle, facing south, to face the threat from Devil's Den. The right flank continued in a failed attempt to support a threatened artillery battery. Flanked

and driven back, they retired in semi-organized order, many men facing about to check the closely following enemy. Retreated to South Cemetery Ridge

Report of Maj. John W. Moore, Ninety-ninth Pennsylvania Infantry.

NEAR WARRENTON, VA., July 27, 1863.

SIR: Early on the morning of the 2d instant, I was ordered to place my regiment in line of battle on the right of the brigade, which formed the extreme left of the line. After lying in this position from two to three hours, I was ordered by General Ward to report with my regiment to Major-General Birney, who in turn ordered me to a position as support to the Third Maine Regiment, which was engaged in skirmishing with the enemy on the Emmitsburg road. This position I held for over an hour, when General Ward advanced the balance of the brigade, joined on my right, changed front, and moved farther to the left, as the enemy was massing his forces and moving on our left flank.

During the afternoon my regiment, with the Twentieth Indiana, was ordered forward through the woods to support Berdan's Sharpshooters. At this time the engagement became very general with the enemy, who was throwing a large force against our brigade, in hopes of breaking through our lines. I was now ordered by General Ward to march my regiment double-quick from the right to the left of the brigade. This movement, rapidly executed, placed my command on the brow of a hill, overlooking a deep ravine interspersed with large bowlders of rock.

Here the conflict was fierce. I held this position for over thirty minutes, until the brigade began to retire on the right, when I ordered the regiment to fall back slowly, covering the rear. General Ward moved the brigade in the rear of General Sykes' division, Fifth Corps, and formed in line of battle. Subsequently I moved with the brigade to the rear, and bivouacked for the night.

UNIT: 110th Infantry. **OTHER NAME:** None.

ORGANIZATION: III Corps, 1st Div., 3rd Brig.

RAISED: From the counties of Blair, Huntingdon, & Philadelphia. **MUSTERED:** Camp Curtin, Harrisburg,

Oct. 24, 1861.

COMMANDER: 1) Lt. Col David M. Jones (1838-1877), wounded on July 2nd. 2) Maj. Isaac Rogers (1834-1864), KIA at Spotsylvania.

MONUMENT LOCATION: A few feet south of DeTrobriand Ave., below the Rocky Knoll near the west branch of Plum Run. The monument represents the advanced position occupied on July 2nd, and the battle line it held as it accepted repeated attacks from Kershaw's Brigade. **MAP:** III, C-1..

STRENGTH: 6 Cos, 152 effectives. **LOSSES:** K-8, W-45, M-0. Total: 53. Percent Loss: 34.9.

WEAPONS: .58 Springfields & .577 Enfields.

SUMMARY: Advanced to the Stony Hill in early afternoon supporting pickets along the Emmitsburg Road. On Longstreet's initial advance, filed to the south and took a defensible position above Plum Run, at site of monument. Repulsed repeated frontal assaults from the direction of the Rose farm, filling the Plum Run ravine to its front and below with piles of dead and wounded from South Carolina. Withdrew as enemy numbers increased, flanking them on the right from where Switzer and Tilton had just withdrawn atop the Stony Hill. Moved east to Cemetery Ridge.

Report of Maj. Isaac Rogers, One hundred and tenth Pennsylvania Infantry. NEAR WARRENTON, VA., August 4, 1863.

SIR: After arriving as far to the front as seemed prudent, the regiment was moved off the road with the brigade in the edge of a woods to the right. At 1 p. m. Lieutenant-Colonel Jones, commanding regiment, was ordered to move forward to a piece of woods and form a line of battle. After this was done, he was ordered to move within supporting distance of our skirmishers, which was promptly and calmly done under fire of artillery. After being in this position until 3.30 p. m., the lieutenant-colonel was ordered by a staff officer to advance 50 paces and join the brigade on the right, under a heavy fire of artillery, which was done with much coolness. After getting established in this position, the skirmishers were driven back, when the general engagement commenced at 4 p. m. Here Lieut. Col. David M. Jones was severely wounded, and the command of the regiment was given over to me. The battle continued with a determination on both sides to conquer or die until 6 p. m., when the enemy in our front fell back, and the order to cease firing was given. This being done, I was ordered by a staff officer to fall back and give place to fresh troops, which was done, moving through a piece of woods, where the brigade was bivouacked for the night. Here my command was prepared for action on the following day. Early on the morning of the 3d, I was ordered to move a short distance to the right, behind a piece of woods and near corps headquarters. After being in this position forty minutes, I was ordered to take up a position on the same ground occupied by this regiment the day before, previous to going into action.

At 1.30 p. m. I was ordered to move forward to a stone fence. Soon after being in this position, I was ordered to change position, and was conducted to the right, behind a battery, where I remained during the afternoon. The fire of the artillery was kept up all afternoon. The casualties in my command, though, were trifling, 2 men being slightly wounded. At 8 p. m. I was ordered to move forward to act as a picket during the night, which was done. Here we remained until morning behind temporary earthworks. My command behaved well during the two days' battle, and as all did well and deserve praise, I will not particularly speak of any one.

UNIT: 115th Infantry. **OTHER NAME:** None.

ORGANIZATION: III Corps, 2nd Div., 3rd Brig.

RAISED: From the counties of Cambria & Philadelphia.
MUSTERED: Hestonville, Philadelphia, January 28, 1862.

COMMANDER: Maj. John P. Dunne (1828-1891).

July 2nd

MONUMENT LOCATION: A simple granite pedestal with a beautiful bronze eagle mounted on top, located on the right shoulder of De Trobriand Ave., in the center of the Rose Woods. The monument represents the approximate advanced position of the regiment after it was detached from its brigade. **MAP:** III, B-2.

STRENGTH: 9 Cos, 151 Effectives. **LOSSES:** K-3, W-18, M-3. Total: 24. Percent Loss: 15.9.

WEAPONS: .577 Enfields.

SUMMARY: Detached from Burling's 3rd Brigade, the 115th, followed by the 8th New Jersey moved south across the Wheatfield in search of Ward's brigade, to which they were being temporarily attached. Ordered to the far southern edge of the Wheatfield, both regiments crossed over the low stone wall and moved into the Rose Woods, the 115th to the left of the 8th. Both units faced due south as Anderson's Georgia Brigade hit them near today's monument from the right oblique. Giving way, the 8th uncovered the 115th's right flank, forcing Maj. Dunne to change direction to the southwest. Slowly forced back by overpowering numbers, the 115th withdrew. Retreated into the Wheatfield, passing through Switzer's advancing brigade. The regiment faced about and knelt down in the wheat, covering the right section of a New York battery, posted on a small knoll in the south center of the Wheatfield. Stood and delivered volleys into Kershaw's men attacking from the Stony Hill. Held their ground as the New Yorker battery pulled their guns back. Moved off the field with the right section, turning about to check the enemy. Retreated northeast over the Wheatfield Road (Fairfield Crossroad) and onto the farm of Jacob Weikert, continuing on to South Cemetery Ridge where they rejoined their brigade.

UNIT: 118th Infantry. **OTHER NAME:** "Corn Exchange Regiment".

ORGANIZATION: V Corps, 1st Div., 1st Brig.

RAISED: Philadelphia. **MUSTERED:** Camp Union, Philadelphia,

Aug. 30, 1862.

COMMANDER: Lt. Col. James B. Gwyn (1828-1906).
MONUMENT LOCATIONS: 1) Sitting in some open woods below the western crest of the Stony Hill, about 40 yards off and below Sickles Ave, above Plum Run. Represents the regiment's apex, or the spot where the line bent back at a ninety degree angle, facing both west and south. 2) Intersection of Wheatfield Road and De Trobriand Ave. 3). Big Round Top. **Map** III, B-1..

STRENGTH: 10 Cos, 233 Effectives. **LOSSES:** K-3, W-19, M-3. Total: 25. Percent Loss: 10.7.

WEAPONS: .58 Springfields.

SUMMARY: Advanced with brigade from the Wheatfield Road, southwest onto the Stony Hill during the initial advance of Longstreet's attack. Took up a line of battle above and to the right rear of the 110th Pa. regiment from DeTrobriand's brigade, covering the right flank of the Stony Hill. The 118th moved past the 110th to a position facing due south, below the crest, just in front of a small copse of trees on top the ridge. Col. Gwyn bent back his right wing to face due west from atop the crest, angling back to the crest with the apex anchored near the small group of trees. The right wing stretched approximately 40 yards north of the present monument, with a clear field of fire to the Sherfy Peach Orchard rise, 400 yards to the west. Helped in the repulse of Anderson's and Kershaw's first attacks, hitting Kershaw's left wing at right enfilade as unexpectedly veered away from the attack and moved toward the Federal batteries posted to the north along the Wheatfield Road. Prematurely withdrew off the Stony Hill, as ordered, moving north with the brigade, firing as they went. Crossed over the Wheatfield Road going into position behind the low stone wall as indicated by present marker, located on the Wheatfield Road at its intersection with Sickles Ave. Briefly held this position, retreating northeast toward the Trostle farm lane and Cemetery Ridge. On the morning of the 3rd ordered to Big Round Top.

UNIT: 62nd Infantry. **OTHER NAME:** "33rd Independent Regiment."
ORGANIZATION: V Corps, 1st Div., 2nd Brig.

RAISED: From the counties of Allegheny, Armstrong, Blair, Clarion & Jefferson. **MUSTERED:** Pittsburgh, July 4,1861.

COMMANDER: Lt. Col. James C. Hull (1827-1864), KIA at Cedar Creek.

MONUMENT LOCATION: On the north shoulder of De Trobriand Ave. near the stone wall separating Rose Woods from the southern edge of the Wheatfield. Monument represents forward position fronting south, moments before moving back to face west. **MAP:** III, B-2.

STRENGTH: 12 Cos, 426 effectives. **LOSSES:** K-28, W-107, M-40, Total: 175. Percent Loss: 41.1.

WEAPONS: .58 Springfields.

SUMMARY: Advanced with the brigade down the Wheatfield Road onto the Stony Hill west of the Wheatfield, and into a position on its crest facing due west. The 62nd helped in the repulse of Kershaw's first attack, being helped when Kershaw's left three regiments unexpectedly turned away from their line and moved north to attack Federal batteries along the Wheatfield Road. On orders, the regiment prematurely moved to the north and off the Stony Hill, crossed the Wheatfield Road, and moved into the smoke-filled Trostle woods, firing as they went. This uncommon move uncovered much of the Stony Hill allowing Kershaw's right regiments a much easier time storming the hill then otherwise would have been allowed.

The 62nd filed east and took cover behind the stone wall bordering the north shoulder of the Wheatfield Road. Again as ordered, the 62nd advanced with the brigade, from the Trostle woods into the Wheatfield toward the stone wall separating the Wheatfield from the Rose woods. The 62nd was the second regiment from the right, going into position at the edge of the Wheatfield near where their monument now stands. Prepared to defend the wall as other Federal regiments withdrew around the brigade. Observing the

Federal withdrawal, Switzer incorrectly assumed they were units that had been relieved, as they were in fact pulling back, with little or no confusion. As the 62nd engaged men from Anderson's and Semmes brigades in the Rose woods, (south) a flank fire from the Stony Hill (right & rear from the west northwest) began to take effect. Ordering the 4th Michigan, posted on the right of the brigade, and the 62nd to change direction, Switzer sent them west toward the Stony Hill. The 62nd advanced approximately 200 yards west of their present monument toward the swampy low ground, with the 4th Michigan still on their right.

Nearly surrounded, the 62nd became embroiled in vicious hand-to-hand combat as Kershaw's men hit them head on. Several bayonet charges were made to drive the Rebels back. Nearly cut off, Col. Hull walked down to what was left of his line, and personally ordered each man out, cutting their way out by the point of the bayonet. Retreated east-northeast each man for himself, past the Valley of Death and onto South Cemetery Ridge.

HEADQUARTERS SECOND BRIGADE, Camp near Warrenton, Va., July 31, 1863.

GENERAL: In obedience to orders, I respectfully submit the following report of the operations of this brigade during the recent battle of Gettysburg:

After a hard march on the day previous, July 1, from Unionville, Md., by way of Hanover, the brigade bivouacked after 12 p. m., with the division in the woods by the roadside, 4 or 5 miles distant from the battle-field.

Next morning by daylight we were on the march again, the Second Brigade leading. Having arrived near what I supposed to be the right of our line, and near a farm-house and barn, the division was massed, the brigades occupying positions in the order of their numbers from right to left, General Sykes' division being on our left. Here a call was made for a regiment from this brigade for picket duty by General Barnes, and Colonel Guiney, with the Ninth Massachusetts, was directed to report to him for instructions, and did so.

Shortly after this, the division changed front to the left, at nearly a right angle with its former position, and formed in line of battalions in close column by division.

We had been in this position but a few moments before we were again moved a considerable distance to the left; then moved by the front across the creek, and massed in an orchard on the hill above the bridge on the Gettysburg turnpike. There we remained until late in the afternoon (the precise time I do not remember), and the command had a few hours' quiet and rest.

Meanwhile there had been very little firing along the line, and I came to the conclusion the day would pass without the division being called into action. But soon after cannonading was heard on the left, and we were moved quite a distance farther to the left, and diagonally to the front, skirting in our march the woods in rear of or in which our lines were formed. When we moved off from the orchard, the Third Brigade, being on the left of the division, moved first, the Second and First Brigades following in the inverted order.

We had not remained long in this position before an attack commenced by the enemy in front of the First Brigade and Thirty-second Massachusetts. As there was no appearance of the enemy in front of the line formed by the Sixty-second Pennsylvania and Fourth Michigan, I directed them to change front to the left, and form lines in rear of the Thirty-second Massachusetts, to strengthen that position. During the execution of this order, the attack continued; the firing was very severe, and we lost many brave officers and men. Here fell Major Lowry, second to none in all the attributes of a soldier and a gentleman.

Some time after that, word was sent that the First Brigade was retiring, and General Barnes sent me word to fall back also, which I did in perfect good order, the regiments retaining their alignments and halting and firing as they came back. Having arrived at the road leading along the rear of the wheat-field, the Brigade was formed in line in the woods in rear of the road and parallel to it, the right resting at the corner of the woods toward the front. We had not remained here more than, say, fifteen minutes, when a general officer I had never seen before rode up to me, and said his command was driving the enemy in the woods in front of the wheat-field and that he needed the support of a brigade and desired to know if I would give him mine.

I referred him to General Barnes, and said I would obey his directions with pleasure. He spoke to the general, who was not far off. General Barnes came and stated to me what had been said to him by General Caldwell (this I learned was the officer who had lately spoken to me), and asked me if I would take the brigade in. I told him I would if he wished me to do so. He said he did. The command was then called to attention. General Barnes got out in front of them, and made a few patriotic remarks, to which they responded with a cheer, and we started off across the wheat-field in a line parallel to the road, our right flank resting in the woods. We advanced to the stone fence beyond the wheat-field next to the woods, and took position behind it to support, as we supposed, our friends in the woods in front. The Fourth Michigan, being on the right of the brigade, extended beyond the stone fence, and was, consequently, most exposed.

We had scarcely got to this position before I noticed regiments retiring from the woods on our right, which I supposed were relieved by others who had taken their places, and would protect us in that direction. I observed also that there was considerable firing diagonally toward our rear from these woods, which I then thought were shots from our troops aimed over us at the enemy in the woods beyond and falling short. They were, however, much too frequent to be pleasant, and my color-bearer, Ed. Martin, remarked, "Colonel, I'll be ———— if I don't think we are faced the wrong way; the rebs are up there in the woods behind us, on the right."

About this time, too, word was brought me from the Fourth Michigan and Sixty-second Pennsylvania that the enemy were getting into our rear in the woods on the right. I directed those regiments to change front, to face in that direction and meet them, which they did, the firing in the meanwhile being rapid and severe. I at the same time dispatched Lieutenant Seitz, aide-de-camp, to communicate to General Barnes our situation. He reached the point where he had last seen General Barnes. He was not there. Lieutenant Seitz found the enemy had reached that point, and he came near falling into their hands himself; his horse was killed, and he made his way back to me on foot; reported that General Barnes was not to be found; that the enemy was in the woods on our right as far back as where we had started from, and along the road in rear of the wheat-field.

Finding that we were surrounded—that our enemy was under cover, while we were in the open field exposed to their fire—I directed the command to fall back. This was done in order, the command halting and firing as it retired. The Fourth Michigan and Sixty-second Pennsylvania had become mixed up with the enemy, and many hand-to-hand conflicts occurred. Colonel Jeffords, the gallant commander of the Fourth Michigan, was thrust through with a bayonet in a contest over his colors, and Sergt. William McFairman, Company I, and Private William McCarter, Company A, Sixty-second Pennsylvania, receive honorable mention by Colonel Hull in his report for their conduct during this part of the engagement.

Finding, as we retired in the direction from which we advanced, that the fire of the enemy grew more severe on our right, I took a diagonal direction toward the corner of the wheat-field on our left and rear. We crossed the stone fence on this side of the field, and retired to the rear of the battery on the elevation beyond, where the command was halted.

We had lost heavily in our passage across the field. The Fourth Michigan and Sixty-second Pennsylvania had been surrounded, and a large proportion of those regiments were missing, either killed, wounded, or prisoners. What remained of the command formed in the rear of the battery, and we were shortly afterward joined by the Ninth Massachusetts, which had been absent all day on detached duty.

It is difficult to conceive of a more trying situation than that in which three regiments of this command had lately found themselves, and from which they had just effected their escape; in fact, I have since understood that one of General Barnes' aides remarked to him shortly after we had advanced, when it was discovered the enemy was behind us on the flank, that he might bid good-bye to the Second Brigade. I was also informed by General Barnes that, learning soon after we had advanced the situation on our right, he had dispatched an orderly to me with the information and a verbal order to withdraw, but the orderly never reached me.

Every officer and man in the command, so far as I am informed, did his whole duty. All stood their ground and fought unflinchingly until they were ordered by me to retire, and in falling back behaved with coolness and deliberation. We lost many of our best officers and men.

UNIT: 83rd Infantry. **OTHER NAME:** None.

ORGANIZATION: V Corps, 1st div., 3rd Brig.

RAISED: From the counties of Crawford, Erie, & Forest.
MUSTERED: Washington D.C., Sept. 8, 1861.

COMMANDER: Capt. Orpheus S. Woodward.

MONUMENT LOCATION: A bronze statue of Capt. Woodward atop a large granite pedestal, 50 yards to the west of Sykes Ave. on an elevated shelf below the southwestern brow of Little Round. **MAP:** III, C-5.

STRENGTH: 10 Cos, 295 Effectives. **LOSSES:** K-10, W-45, M-0, Total: 55. Percent Loss: 18.6.

WEAPONS: .58 Springfields.

SUMMARY: Arrived on the southwest brow of Little Round Top with little time to build fortifications. Skirmishers sent forward toward today's Warren Ave., were met at once by enemy skirmishers, followed by a battle line with fixed bayonets. Retreated until left flank met the right of the 20th Maine near today's Sykes Ave., facing due south. It ran west toward today's monument where it bent back at slight right angles to face west-southwest, toward the Slaughter Pen at the intersection of today's Crawford and Warren Avenues. Accepted continued charges from the 4th Texas and 47th Alabama, inflicting and suffering heavy casualties. Vicious hand-to-hand fighting ensued as the Texans attempted to breech the right flank, which nearly succeeded, but again were repulsed with terrible losses. Counter-charged after seeing the success of the 20th Maine's desperate charge down the saddle in front of their left flank. Collected many prisoners. Remained in this position until after midnight when it filed to the crest of Big Round Top.

Report of Capt. Orpheus S. Woodward, Eighty-third Pennsylvania Infantry. NEAR EMMITSBURG, MD., July 6, 1863.

LIEUTENANT: At about 2.30 p. m. was ordered into position on our extreme left, the Forty-fourth New York on my right the Twentieth Maine on my left. At 3.15 p. m. the enemy advanced and engaged my skirmishers, pressing on in force, with bayonets fixed. They soon drove in my skirmishers and engaged my regiment, posted behind rocks and stones hastily thrown up for defense. The contest continued lively until nearly 6 p. m., when the enemy fell back. I instantly threw forward a strong line of skirmishers, who captured between 50 and 60 prisoners and 250 stand of arms.

My men and officers acted splendidly. Where all did so well, I cannot discriminate.

At 1.30 a. m. on the 3d, moved to the support of the Twentieth Maine, which had succeeded in taking a high hill a little to the left of my former position. Remained here until 10 a. m., when, being relieved by a regiment of the Pennsylvania Reserves, rejoined my brigade, massed in the woods, just at the right of General Sykes' headquarters. Here I remained until 12 m., the 4th, when the brigade was thrown forward on a reconnaissance. I regret to state that Colonel Vincent was severely wounded. My command (his regiment) esteemed him highly as a gentleman, scholar, and soldier, and bitterly avenged his injury

UNIT: 91st Infantry. **OTHER NAME:** None.

July 2nd

ORGANIZATION: V Corps, 2nd div., 3rd Brig.

RAISED: Philadelphia county.
MUSTERED: Camp Chase, Philadelphia. Dec., 4, 1861.

COMMANDER: Lt. Col. Joseph H. Sinex (1819-1892).

MONUMENT LOCATION: On the crest and west brow of Little Round Top. **MAP:** III, C-5.

STRENGTH: 10 Cos, 219 Effectives. **LOSSES:** K-3, W-16, M-0. Total: 19. Percent Loss: 8.7.

WEAPONS: .58 Springfields.

SUMMARY: Advanced west past the George Weikert farm, located at the present day intersection of Hancock and U. S. Avenues, in a vain attempt to help support the 5th U. S. Battery I (Watson) which sat engaged just east of the Trostle Farm. As ordered, followed the 140th New York south down a small farm lane, moving off the road as two V Corps batteries (Walcott & Hazlett) raced by toward the Jacob Weikert farm and the Valley of Death. Turned east on the Wheatfield Road, then back south on the present Sykes Ave. Climbed the east slope of Little Round Top, going into position on the right of the 140th New York, and to the left of a section of cannons (5th U.S.Battery D) going into position on the crest. Helped in the repulse of the 48th Alabama and the 4th Texas. Held this position throughout the remainder of the battle. Not actively engaged. Details helped bury the dead that laid throughout the Valley of Death as well as Little Round Top.

UNIT: 155th Infantry. **OTHER NAME:** None.

ORGANIZATION: V Corps, 2nd Div., 3rd Brig.

RAISED: From the counties of Allegheny, Armstrong, & Clarion. **MUSTERED:** Camp Howell, Pittsburgh. Sept. 2,

1862.

COMMANDER: Lt. Col. John H. Cain (1838-1903).

MONUMENT LOCATION: Granite statue of a Zouave infantryman confidently ramming home a round. Located on the north shoulder, 100 yards north and below the crest of Little Round Top approximately 75 yards due west of Sykes Ave. **MAP:** III, B-6.

STRENGTH: 10 Cos, 360 effectives. **LOSSES:** K-6, W-13, M-0, Total: 19. Percent Loss: 5.3.

WEAPONS: .69 smoothbores.

SUMMARY: Advanced west past the George Weikert farm, located at the intersection of Hancock and U.S. Avenues on south Cemetery Ridge, in a vain attempt to reach and support the 5th U.S. Battery I (Watson) now engaged just east of the Trostle farm above the Plum Run. As ordered, moved to the left (south) following a small farm lane (the lane that once connected the Jacob and George Weikert farms) toward today's Valley of Death. Moved off the lane as the 3rd Massachusetts battery (Walcott) and the 5th U.S. Battery D (Hazlett) raced by. Turned east on the Wheatfield Road, near present day Crawford Ave., and proceeded up the Wheatfield road, turning back south on present Sykes Ave. Went into position at present monument under heavy musketry from the southwest, as the 4th Texas and 48th Alabama attempted to flank the Federal right. Held this line after reconstructing breastworks for the remainder of the battle. Not engaged on July 3rd. Helped in the burying of dead and the destruction of enemy arms.

UNIT: 81st Infantry. **OTHER NAME:** None.

ORGANIZATION: II Corps. 1st Div., 1st Brig.

RAISED: From the counties of Carbon, Luzerne, & Philadelphia. **MUSTERED:** Camp Worth, Philadelphia,

Aug., 1861.

COMMANDER: Lt. Col. Amos Stoh (1821-1899).

MONUMENT LOCATION: Fifty yards due west of Ayres Ave. in the Wheatfield. Represents their line of battle during the engagement. **MAP:** III, B-2.

STRENGTH: 10 Cos, 175 effectives. **LOSSES:** K-6, W-49, M-8. Total: 62. Percent Loss: 35.4.

WEAPONS: .58 Springfields & .69 Smoothbores.

SUMMARY: Advanced with the brigade, leading the way, southwest toward the Wheatfield, a distance of nearly one-half mile, moving in column by the left flank across today's United States Avenue, and into the Trostle woods beyond. Dressed their ranks in the woods behind the stone and rail fence on the north shoulder of the Wheatfield Road. As ordered, jumped over the fence with the brigade, redressed ranks in the road, and with a cheer charged due south into the Wheatfield. Advanced two thirds of the way across the field when extreme fire from Rebels behind the stone wall bordering the eastern Wheatfield erupted with devastating effect. Stood, anchoring the brigade's right flank, on a little knoll in the open, firing toward the stone wall and Rose woods 100 yards south of their present monument. Retired when flanked and driven back, with ammunition nearly exhausted. Reassembled northeast of the Jacob Weikert farm yard, withdrew to Cemetery Ridge. Held in reserve in rear of McGilvery's artillery line, not engaged on July 3rd. One casualty reported killed during the great cannonade on July 3rd.

Report of Lieut. Col. Amos Stroh, Eighty-first Pennsylvania Infantry.
NEAR GETTYSBURG, PA., July 6,1863.
  SIR: About seven o'clock on the evening of the 2d instant, we were moved to the left, where we found a heavy infantry fight going on. We took our position on a knoll in an open

field, on the edge of which the enemy lay, under cover of a stone wall and partly concealed by a dense wood. Here we opened fire, and expended nearly all our ammunition, when we were relieved by another regiment taking our place. We lay on the field a short time, and then marched still farther to the rear, and took position with the One hundred and forty-eighth-Pennsylvania Volunteers behind a stone fence, where we were joined by the balance of the brigade, and marched back to the position we occupied in the early part of the day, and which we still occupy. Compared to the number we took into action, our loss was nearly as great as in any former engagement.

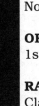

UNIT: 148th Infantry. **OTHER NAME:** None.

ORGANIZATION: II Corps, 1st Div., 1st Brig.

RAISED: From the Counties of Centre, Clarion, & Jefferson. **MUSTERED:** Camp Curtin, Harrisburg, Sept. 1, 1862.

COMMANDER: 1) Col. Henry B. McKeen (1835-1864), assumed command of brigade on Colonel Cross' wounding (KIA at Cold Harbor). 2) Lt. Col. Robert McFarland (1826-1891), assumed command on McKeen's field promotion.

MONUMENT LOCATION: 10 yards due south of Ayres Ave. in the Wheatfield (near the loop). The monument represents the battle line held during the engagement. **MAP:** III, B-2.

STRENGTH: 10 Cos, 392 effectives. **LOSSES:** K-19, W-101, M-5, Total: 125. Percent Loss: 31.9.

WEAPONS: .58 Springfields.

SUMMARY: Advanced nearly one-half mile with the brigade from Cemetery Ridge southwest toward the Wheatfield, moving in column by the left flank. Entered the Trostle woods after crossing present U.S. Ave. and continuing south across the Plum Run. Dressed their lines in the woods behind the stone and rail fence bordering the east shoulder of the Wheatfield Road (directly north of the present day Wheatfield Road &. Ayres Ave. intersection). As ordered, jumped over the fence, redressing their ranks in the road, and with a cheer charged with the brigade into the field. Their route was due south following the present day Ayres Ave. as it runs south toward the Rose woods, 400 yards away. Heavy frontal fire forced the regiment into a firing line 100 yards from a stone wall and the Rose woods, the left wing extending into a portion of the Rose woods itself, while the right wing stood in the open on the southeast face of a small knoll in the Wheatfield. Extreme enemy pressure forced the right wing back as the left wing took possession of the stone wall (40 yards northeast of the monument) forcing back the Confederates. Mounting pressure on the right forced an orderly withdrawal, as the left moved back firing, covering the withdrawal of the right. Hand-to-hand combat ensued as the color company attempted to retreat with their flag. Withdrew in order, when relieved by V Corps units. Retreated back to the Jacob Weikert farm yard, reorganized, and pulled back with the brigade to Cemetery Ridge, just south of the today's Pennsylvania monument.

UNIT: 116th Infantry. **OTHER NAME:** None.

ORGANIZATION: II Corps, 1st Div., 3rd Brigd.

RAISED: Philadelphia. **MUSTERED:** Camp Emmet, Philadelphia, Sept., 1st, 1862.

COMMANDER: Maj. St. Clair Augustin Mulholland (1839-1910).

MONUMENT LOCATION: Just northwest of Sickles Ave. on the crest of the Stony Hill where the road makes it loop. The monument represents the battle line held but not their farthest advance. **MAP:** III, A-1.

STRENGTH: Three companies. A, B, C & D (temporarily detached), 66 effectives. **LOSSES:** K-2, W-11, M-9. Total: 22. Percent Loss: 33.3.

WEAPONS: .69 Smoothbores.

SUMMARY: Moved with the brigade from Cemetery Ridge southwest toward the Wheatfield, approximately one half mile. Moved into line of battle, anchoring the right flank of the 3rd (Irish) Brigade, in the Trostle woods behind the stone wall bordering the northern shoulder of the Wheatfield Road. As ordered, jumped the wall, redressed ranks in the road, and charged into the wheat, moving to the south-southwest toward the low marshy ground and the Stony Hill. Scaled the Stony Ridge at the southwestern edge of the Wheatfield, 30 yards west of today's monument to the Irish Brigade, located on Sickles Ave. Advanced onto the crest where as they met frontal fire from a formed enemy line. Basically attached to the right of the 28th Massachusetts, the few men from the 116th held their ground near their present day monument, firing to the southwest and the Plum Run. On orders, joined the 28th in a bayonet charge toward the Plum Run, 40 yards west of their present day monument. Moved off the Stony Hill with the brigade as it swept forward into the Plum Run and on toward the Rose farm, another 200 yards to the west-southwest. Stalled on the west bank of the run by enemy reinforcements, the 116th pulled back, with the brigade, into a better defensive position on top of the Stony Hill at the site of their monument, and held their ground, accepting repeated charges from the Rose farm. Flanked on the right and rear, they withdrew back through the Wheatfield toward the Jacob Weikert farm, then on to Cemetery Ridge. Held in reserve in rear of McGilvery's line on July 3rd, not engaged.

Report of Maj. St. Clair A. Mulholland, One hundred and sixteenth Pennsylvania Infantry. IN CAMP, SANDY HOOK, MD., JULY 17, 1863.

SIR: Shortly after daybreak on the morning of the 2d, in compliance with orders received, the brigade of which my regiment has the honor of being a part moved up to a field within sight of the enemy's pickets. Our division was deployed in mass in column of regiments, my regiment being placed in the front line. Here we stacked arms, and ordered the men to rest. We remained in this position during the forenoon of the 2d instant. Heavy firing was heard at intervals on our right during the day, although everything remained quiet in the vicinity of my command until about 3 p.m.

About this time firing commenced on our left, I think about three-fourths of a mile distant. The firing had continued about an hour when orders came for us to fall in. We at once took up arms, and were marched by the left flank toward the scene of action. After marching nearly 1 mile, and the division being in line of battle, we advanced to support (I think) a portion of the Third Army Corps, which was then engaged. The brigade to which we are attached advanced in line of battle, left in front, gallantly led by Col. P. Kelly, of the Eighty-eighth New York Volunteers. As we advanced, portions of the Third Corps retired, passing through the intervals of our line. Having entered a dense woods, we began to ascend a hill, where large boulders of rocks impeded our progress, notwithstanding which we advanced in good order. We soon came within sight of the enemy, who occupied the crest of the hill, and who immediately opened fire at our approach. Our brigade returned the fire with good effect. After firing for about ten minutes, the order was given to advance, which the brigade did in excellent style, driving the enemy from their position, which we at once occupied. We took many prisoners at this point, hundreds of the enemy laying down their arms and passing to the rear. We found the position which our foes had occupied but a few moments before thickly strewn with the dead and wounded. Here we again opened fire, the enemy having rallied to oppose our farther advance. After being engaged for about twenty minutes and the enemy having been re-enforced, the division began to retire in good order. At this time the division was completely outflanked by the enemy, who had formed a line facing the right flank of our brigade. This line was formed along the edge of a wheat-field, about a quarter of a mile in rear of our brigade. This field we had to cross to get to the rear. In doing so, we encountered the full sweep of the enemy's fire, which at this point was most destructive. Many of the division fell before this terrible fire.

Shortly after dark we were again marched to the

front, and placed in the same position that we had occupied in the morning. Here we lay on our arms all night, and were awakened at daybreak by the sound of the enemy's cannon. Major-General Hancock passed along early in the day, and moved our line a little forward, in order that we might have a better range and our fire be more effective, should the enemy attack us. We immediately commenced to intrench our new position, and by 11 a.m. had quite a formidable breastwork thrown up. All this forenoon we could see the enemy preparing to attack us. Several batteries were placed in position opposite our line, and everything indicated that an attack was intended.

About noon the attack commenced by a most terrific shelling of our lines by the enemy, but, thanks to our earthworks and the inaccurate aim of the gunners, none of my command were injured. After shelling our position for about two hours, the fire of the artillery somewhat slackened, and a heavy force of rebel infantry was seen advancing upon our works. At this moment our artillery, which up to this time had remained almost silent, opened with terrible effect upon the advancing lines, tearing great gaps in their ranks and strewing the field with dead and wounded. Notwithstanding the destructive fire under which they were placed, the enemy continued to advance with a degree of ardor, coolness, and bravery worthy of a better cause, until, reaching a ravine which ran parallel with our line, about midway between us and their artillery, they halted, being under cover and no longer exposed to our fire. They halted but to surrender. Finding, I presume, that their ranks were too much thinned to think of charging our works, knowing the heavy loss they would sustain in attempting to reach their own lines again, and thinking discretion the better part of valor, they laid down their arms and surrendered almost to a man. Perceiving the failure of their infantry to carry our position, the enemy again opened their batteries, but, after another hour's fire, withdrew, leaving us victors of the field.

During the day's fighting the heat was very great, and the men, being exposed and having neither shelter nor water, suffered intensely. Soon after sunset the same evening the rain commenced to descend in torrents, wetting every one, filling the rifle-pits, and making us most uncomfortable. But my command was ever hopeful, and bore the fatigue and suffering incidental to a great battle with the cheerfulness that ever characteristizes the true soldier.

In closing my report, I cannot refrain from mentioning the cool and gallant bearing of my command. Of the officers it is almost useless for me to speak. Every one did his duty in a manner that excited my warmest admiration and gratitude. Were I to mention any one in particular it would be but showing injustice to the rest, as each one tried to excel the other in deeds of gallantry and daring. Of the enlisted men, I feel happy in mentioning the names of Color Sergt. Abraham T. Detweiler, Sergt. Thomas Detweiler, Company A, and Private Jefferson Carl, Company C, as having especially distinguished themselves in the action of the 2d instant

UNIT: 140th Infantry. **OTHER NAME:** None.

ORGANIZATION: II Corps, 1st Div., 3rd Brig.

RAISED: From the counties of Beaver, Greene, Mercer, & Washington.
MUSTERED: Camp Curtin, Harrisburg, Sept., 4,1862.

COMMANDER: 1) Col.Richard P. Roberts (1820-1863), killed July 2nd on the Stony Hill. 2) Lt. Col. James Fraser (1827-1878).

MONUMENT LOCATIONS: 1) On the east shoulder of Sickles Ave. atop the crest of the Stony Hill. 2) About 100 feet west of Sickles Ave., and 40 yards west of the No. 1 monument, below the west brow of the Stony Hill. The monuments represent the advanced position occupied by the regiment, and the death of Col. Roberts. **MAP:** III, B-1.

STRENGTH: 10 Cos, 515 effectives. **LOSSES:** K-37, W-69, M-60. Total: 24. Percent Loss: 46.8.

WEAPONS: .58 Springfields.

SUMMARY: As ordered, advanced with the brigade from

Cemetery Ridge southwest toward the Wheatfield. Moved through the Trostle woods after crossing present United States Avenue, and Plum Run. Dressed ranks behind the stone wall located on the southern edge of the Trostle woods, bordering today's Wheatfield Road. Jumped the wall and redressed ranks in the road before charging into the Wheatfield oblique to the road. Slowly advanced, anchoring the right flank of the 3rd (Zook's) Brigade, toward the southwest and the Stony Hill, driving the enemy back before them. Formed a firing line on top of the crest of the Stony Hill at the present site of the No. 1 monument, slowly moving forward toward the Plum Run, and the position occupied by the No. 2 monument. Actively engaged the enemy attacking from the Rose Farm to the southwest, and a new column from due west, attacking from the Sherfy Peach Orchard. Pulled back the right companies at right angles to meet this new threat, holding their position on the southwest, and west brow of the Stony Hill. The 140th held its position as its left became embroiled in hand-to-hand combat as regiments on their left melted away. The right wing moved back firing as it withdrew, following present Wheatfield Road, back toward the Jacob Weikert farm, as the left wing was swept off the Hill into the Wheatfield in confusion. Nearly engulfed by pursuing Confederates, the survivors cut their way out with clubbed muskets. Reassembled near the Weikert farm and moved back to Cemetery Ridge. Held in reserve in rear of McGilvery's line on July 3rd.

Report of Lt. Col. John Fraser, 140th Pennsylvania. HEADQUARTERS 140TH PENNSYLVANIA VOLUNTEERS, August 7, 1863.

CAPTAIN: About 4 p.m. the brigade was marched rapidly to the left, to assist the Third Corps, which was then sustaining a fierce attack. When it arrived nearly opposite the place assigned to it, the brigade was formed in line of battle, with the One hundred and fortieth Pennsylvania Volunteers on the extreme right, and was moved rapidly forward to engage the enemy. As soon as the order was given, this regiment opened a brisk fire, which it kept up with great firmness and coolness, steadily driving the enemy before it until we reached the crest of a small hill. During the advance to this crest, the four left companies of this regiment, with the regiments to the left, gradually made a considerable wheel to the right. Shortly after reaching the crest, I observed a great many to the left of this brigade moving rapidly to the rear, and the rebels, apparently fresh troops, in large numbers and in good order marching to outflank us on the right. Anxious to know what orders General Zook had to give in the crisis, I sent twice to get instructions from him, but neither the general nor any of his staff could be found. I did not know at the time, nor until after the fight was over, that General Zook had been mortally wounded when leading the brigade into action. Inferring, from the large numbers of men who to the left of my regiment were continuously rushing to the rear, that a large portion of our division was actually retreating, I judged it necessary for the safety of those who had wheeled considerably into the enemy's ground to maintain my position and keep the enemy at bay as long as possible. I therefore held my position until I considered it necessary to order my men to march in retreat, which they did at first in good order, the four right companies halting several times, and firing, to check the pursuit of the enemy.

After this engagement on the 2d, the regiment assembled with the rest of the brigade, and formed in line of battle on the left center of the battle-ground and about 50 paces in rear of the Second Brigade.

On the morning of July 3, the regiment, pursuant to orders, constructed breastworks immediately in front of its line. The severe and long-continued artillery fire which the rebels opened upon us prior to their fruitless attack upon our position in the afternoon of this day, did no harm to any one in the regiment.

Colonel Roberts was killed while bravely leading on his men at the commencement of the action on July 2. The conduct of officers and men in these engagements at Gettysburg deserves the highest praise. A list of the heavy casualties of the regiment has been already forwarded.

UNIT: 53rd Infantry. **OTHER NAME:** None.

ORGANIZATION: II Corps. 1st Div., 4th Brig.

RAISED: From the counties of Juniata, Luzerne, Montgomery, Northumberland, Potter, & Westmorland.
MUSTERED: Camp Curtin, Harrisburg, Nov. 7, 1861.

COMMANDER: Lt. Col. Richard McMicheal (1816-1894).

MONUMENT LOCATION: On the east shoulder of Brooks Ave. in the Rose Woods above Plum Run. Represents the advanced position held during their engagement. **MAP:** III, C-1.

STRENGTH: 7 Cos (A, B, & K detached), 135 effectives. **LOSSES:** K-7, W-67, M-6. Total: 80. Percent Loss: 59.3.

WEAPONS: .58 Springfields.

SUMMARY: Advanced by the left flank with the brigade from Cemetery Ridge toward the Wheatfield. Crossed into the Trostle woods via today's U.S. Ave. east of Plum Run. Dressed ranks behind the stone wall in the southern edge of the Trostle woods bordering the Wheatfield Road. Crossed over the wall and redressed ranks in the road before charging into the wheat. Advanced in the center of the brigade to the middle of the Wheatfield and formed a firing line. On orders, fixed bayonets and charged into the Rose woods driving the enemy before them. Moved rapidly across Sickles Ave. heading southwest toward the Plum Run capturing many prisoners. Crossed the gully of the Plum Run and scaled the precipitous west bank going into position at the site of their monument along Brooke Ave. Held this position as Confederate reinforcements attacked from the Emmitsburg Road in overpowering numbers. Did not withdraw until flanked and out of ammunition. Contested every foot of ground until the Wheatfield was reached. Once there the regiment, as others, fell into confusion as they made their dash back toward the Wheatfield Road and the Jacob Weikert farm. Reassembled and moved back to Cemetery Ridge.

Report Lt. of Col. R. McMichael, Commdg. Fifty-third Pennsylvania Infnatry. HDQRS. FIFTY-THIRD PENNSYLVANIA VOLUNTEERS, near Morrisville, Va., August 14, 1863.

SIR: At daybreak on the 2d, I withdrew the pickets, in accordance with the orders of Colonel Brooke, commanding brigade, and, falling into my assigned position in line of march, moved toward Gettysburg, arriving on the field about 8 a.m. I was marched to a position in the rear of the left center of the line of battle then forming, where I remained about one hour, when my command was marched to a position on the front line. I remained in this position midafternoon, when the action commenced. For several hours I remained inactive under a severe shelling from the guns of the enemy.

About 5 p.m., in compliance with orders from Colonel Brooke, commanding brigade, I, in connection with the brigade, moved by the left flank toward the left of the line, and formed in line of battle near a grain-field. The Sixty-fourth New York was on my right and the Twenty-seventh Connecticut on my left. In accordance with the orders of the brigade commander, I fixed bayonets, and, in line with the rest of the brigade, charged upon the enemy. The rebels gave way; were forced from a strong position on the crest of a hill in our immediate front. The position was held until the enemy commenced to mass heavy columns on our flanks for the purpose of cutting us off; then, in compliance with orders of Colonel Brooke, I retired, halting and reforming near Round Top hill.

UNIT: 145th Infantry. **OTHER NAME:** None.

ORGANIZATION: II Corps, 1st Div., 4th Brig.

RAISED: From the counties of Crawford, Erie, Mercer, & Warren. **MUSTERED:** Erie County Fairgrounds, Erie. Sept., 5, 1862.

COMMANDER: 1) Col. Hiram L. Brown (1832-1880), wounded in the Wheatfield on July 2nd. 2) Capt. John W. Reynolds (1836-1925), wounded in the Rose woods on July 2nd. 3) Capt. Moses W. Oliver (1833-1906), assumed command on Reynolds' wounding.

MONUMENT LOCATION: On the east shoulder of Brooke

Ave. in the Rose Woods west of the Plum Run. **MAP:** III, C-1.

STRENGTH: 10 Cos, 202 effectives. **LOSSES:** K-11, W-69, M-10. Total: 90. Percent Loss: 44.6.

WEAPONS: .69 Smoothbores.

SUMMARY: Advanced with the brigade from Cemetery Ridge southwest toward the Wheatfield. Moved through the Trostle Woods via U.S. Ave. east of Plum Run, to the stone wall bordering the Wheatfield Road on the southern edge of the woods. Charged into the Wheatfield and formed a firing line on the small knoll in the center of the wheat, taking many casualties. On orders, charged the stone wall bordering the southern edge of the Wheatfield, driving the enemy beyond it. Advanced with the bayonet into the Rose woods moving to the southwest, continuing to drive the Rebel line back. Crossed over the Plum Run gully, and west up its precipitous embankment. Formed a firing line at the site of today's monument, holding this position until flanked and themselves driven back. Withdrew into the Wheatfield taking many casualties, continuing back toward the Jacob Weikert farm. Withdrew to Cemetery ridge in disorder. Held in reserve in rear of McGilvery's artillery line.

Report of Capt. John W. Reynolds, One hundred and forty-fifth Pennsylvania Infantry. HEADQUARTERS 145TH PENNSYLVANIA VOLUNTEERS, August 14, 1863.

DEAR SIR: The next morning (July 2), we moved forward at daylight about 2 miles, and turned to the right into the woods, where we halted and formed into column by division. Remaining about an hour, the command "Attention" was given, and the regiment moved out to the road again, which we crossed, and, having advanced a short distance, we formed in line of battle in the rear of the brigade, which was then in column by regiments, holding a position a short distance to the left of Cemetery Hill. Having stacked arms, we remained here until about 4 o'clock in the afternoon, when we moved by the left flank about a quarter of a mile, but soon returned again to our former position. About 5 o'clock we were again ordered to march by the left flank. We moved half a mile to the left and formed in line of battle, faced by the rear rank, the brigade forming a single line of battle; our regiment, on the left, now became the right. We lay down for a short time, and then moved forward into a wheat-field, halted, and commenced firing. Soon Colonel Brown was severely wounded and left the field, and, being the senior officer present, I assumed command of the regiment.

About this time the order was given to move forward, and we advanced rapidly with the rest of the brigade for several hundred yards, the enemy retreating, until we came to a ledge of rocks; here a number of the rebels threw down their arms and surrendered, passing to our rear. We continued firing at this point for twenty minutes, when we received an order to fall back. The enemy was already attempting to turn our flank, and had we remained much longer we would have been taken prisoners. The regiment retired, and again took the position that it had occupied during the day. Having received a slight wound in the head, I went to the hospital, and the command of the regiment devolved upon Captain Oliver.

On Friday, the regiment built a line of intrenchments just in front of its position occupied on Thursday, and lay there all day, subject to a severe fire from the enemy's artillery for several hours. At 4 p.m. a detail for picket was sent to the front and deployed as skirmishers; 1 man was wounded.

UNIT: 26th Infantry. **OTHER NAME:** None.

ORGANIZATION: III Corps, 2nd Div., 1st Brig.

RAISED: Philadelphia. **MUSTERED:** May 27, 1862.

COMMANDER: Maj. Robert L. Bodine (1832-1874).

MONUMENT LOCATION: On the east shoulder of the Emmitsburg Road approximately 400 yards north of its intersection with

Sickles Ave. The monument represents the regiment's forward position on July 2nd as they prepared to accept the attack from Wilcox's and Lang's brigades. **MAP:** V, E-2..

STRENGTH: 10 Cos, 365 effectives. **LOSSES:** K-30, W-176, M-7. Total: 213. Percent Loss: 58.4.

WEAPONS: .54 Austrians.

SUMMARY: On Longstreet's attack, the regiment was forced to withdraw, taking heavy casualties as its left flank was rolled up. Changed directions to the southwest on the retreat, facing about to check the advancing enemy on several occasions. An ill-fated but determined counter-charge succeeded in the capture of one enemy color (see M.O.H., Sgt. George Roosevelt), suffering more casualties than inflicted. Retreated back to Cemetery Ridge.

Report of Maj. Robert L. Bodine, Twenty-sixth Pennsylvania Infantry. Camp near Warrenton, VA., July 28, 1863.

Captain: On the morning of July 2, my regiment was detailed to clear away the fences in front of the division, to facilitate the movements of our troops. It was soon after deployed to the right of the brigade, which position it held during the battle, in which I lost many valuable officers and enlisted men. We bivouacked on the battle-field during the night. Next morning, 3d, again prepared for battle, but were not so much engaged or losses so heavy.

I cannot close this report without mentioning with pride the gallant conduct and bravery of my officers in the late battle of Gettysburg, and for the alacrity and willingness displayed in seconding their superiors in their efforts to make the contest a decisive one and do honor to our native State, the old Keystone. The men were also unusually anxious to meet the enemy, and seemed inspired with a feeling to do or die in the attempt to annihilate the invaders of their homes.

UNIT: 11th Reserves. **OTHER NAME:** "40th Infantry."

ORGANIZATION: V Corps, 3rd div., 3rd Brig.

RAISED: From the counties of Armstrong, Butler,

July 2nd

Cambria, Fayette, Indiana, Jefferson, & Westmoreland. **MUSTERED:** Camp Wright, Pittsburgh, June 29, 1861.

COMMANDER: Col. Samuel M. Jackson (1833-1907).

MONUMENT LOCATION: In the Wheatfield a few feet southeast of the intersection of Ayres Ave. and the Wheatfield Road. The monument represents the regiment's advanced position on its charge into the Wheatfield. **MAP:** III, A-3.

STRENGTH: 10 Cos, 327 effectives. **LOSSES:** K-3, W-38, M-0. Total: 41. Percent Loss: 12.5.

WEAPONS: .69 rifled Springfields.

SUMMARY: Detached from the 3rd Brigade, the 11th aligned itself between the 1st and 6th Reserves from McCandless' 1st Brigade and advanced from Little Round Top 700 yards toward the Wheatfield. As the 6th obliqued to the northwest across the Wheatfield Road, the 11th continued due west, its right flank on or near the Wheatfield Road. Advanced to the stone wall that bordered the eastern edge of the Wheatfield, 100 yards east of their present monument. Contested the wall in hand-to-hand combat, driving the few remaining Confederates back into the wheat. On orders, crossed over the wall and continued to press the retreating enemy back toward the Stoney Hill. Enfilading crossfire drove the regiment back to the stone wall where it secured its position for the remainder of July 2nd.

UNIT: 1st Reserves **OTHER NAME:** "30th Infantry."

ORGANIZATION: V Corps, 3rd Div, 2nd Brig.

RAISED: From the counties of Adams, Chester, Cumberland, & Delaware (Co K from the Gettysburg Area). **MUSTERED:** Camp near Hestonville, Philadelphia, July 17, 1861.

COMMANDER: Col. William C. Talley (1831-1903).

MONUMENT'S & LOCATION FOR JULY 2ND: Located on the eastern edge of the Wheatfield off the right shoulder of Ayres Ave., approximately 50 yards south of the Wheatfield Road. Monument represents the farthest advanced position before being flanked and nearly surrounded. **MAP:** III, A-3.

STRENGTH: 10 Cos, 377 effectives. **LOSSES:** K-8, W-38, M-0, Total-46 Percent Loss-12.2.

WEAPONS: .69 rifled Springfields.

SUMMARY: Advanced west from the ridge north of Little Round Top to the stone wall bordering the eastern edge of the Wheatfield, 700 yards distant. Anchoring the the left flank of the first line of battle, the regiment took heavy casualties from enfilading fire from the woods atop Houck's Ridge. On reaching the wall they engaged in hand-to-hand combat, driving the enemy back into the wheat. Advanced over the wall driving the enemy back toward the Stoney Hill, to the position of their present-day monument. A heavy enfilading and frontal fire drove the regiment back to the stone wall where they remained for the remainder of July 2nd.

UNIT: 2nd Reserves. **OTHER NAME:** "31st Infantry".

ORGANIZATION: V Corps, 3rd Div., 1st Brig.

RAISED: Philadelphia. **MUSTERED:** Camp Washington, Easton, May, 27, 1861.

COMMANDER: Lt. Col. George A. Woodward (1835-1916).

MONUMENT LOCATION: On the east shoulder of Ayres Ave.

located in the Wheatfield, south of the 1st Reserve monument, and 100 yards south of the Wheatfield Road. Monument represents farthest advanced position. **MAP:** III, B-3..

STRENGTH: 9 Cos, 232 effectives. **LOSSES:** K-3, W-33, M-1. Total: 37. Percent Loss: 15.9.

WEAPONS: .577 Enfields & .69 rifled Springfields.

SUMMARY: Advanced in second line with brigade from the Little Round Top, 700 yards west to the stone wall separating the Valley of Death from the eastern edge of the Wheatfield. Obliqued to the left and went into position on left of the 1st Reserves, where hand-to-hand combat ensued for possession of the wall. On orders, the regiment charged over the wall into the Wheatfield driving the enemy back. Outflanked and nearly surrounded, the regiment pulled back to the wall, retreating in line of battle, holding that position for the remainder of July 2nd.

Report of Col. William McCandless, Second Pennsylvania Reserves, Commanding First Brigade. HDQRS, FIRST BRIGADE, PENNSYLVANIA RESERVES, Near South Mountain, July 9, 1863.

SIR: After a week of continuous marching, the command arrived on the field about 1 p. m. of the 2d instant, and at 6 p. m. was assigned a position near the left, that being the point against which the enemy had massed a heavy force.

Our first position was naturally strong, being a rocky, wooded hillside, with good cover, sloping steeply down to a plain, which extended from the base about 700 yards to a stone wall. This plain was marshy and difficult to cross over it, however, the enemy passed his infantry in a disordered mass, driving our forces back on my position.

I immediately formed my brigade, together with the Eleventh Regiment of the Third Brigade, in two lines, the first line being composed of the Sixth Regiment on the right, the First on the left, and the Eleventh in the center. The second line was massed on the first, and was composed of the First Rifles (Bucktails) and Second Regiment of Infantry. As soon as our front was uncovered, the brigade advanced in gallant style, the first line delivering one volley, then the whole brigade charged at a full run down the hillside and across the plain, driving the advancing masses of the enemy back upon the stone wall, for the possession of which there was a desperate struggle, we finally carrying it. Prior to reaching the wall, however, my left flank being exposed to a galling fire, I deployed the second line, viz, the First Rifles and Second Regiment, to the left, forming a prolongation of my first line, along with which they steadily advanced. It was at this time, and when within a short distance of the wall, that the brave and lamented Col. Charles F. Taylor fell, while gallantly leading his regiment.

Being ordered not to advance beyond the stone wall, I formed a line along it, threw a strong line of skirmishers on my front, and flankers on my right and left. I remained in this position up to 6 p.m.

UNIT: 5th Reserves. **OTHER NAME:** "31st Infantry."

ORGANIZATION: V Corps, 3rd Div., 3rd Brig.

RAISED: From the counties of Bradford, Centre, Clearfield, Huntingdon, Lancaster, Lycoming, Northumberland, & Union.
MUSTERED: Camp Curtin, Harrisburg, June 20, 1861.

COMMANDER: Lt. Col. George Dare (1836-1864), KIA at the Wilderness.

MONUMENT LOCATION: On the crest of Big Round Top.
MAP: III, F-4.

STRENGTH: 10 Cos, 284 effectives. **LOSSES:** K-0, W-2, M-0. Total: 2. Percent Loss: .7.

WEAPONS: .69 Smoothbores.

SUMMARY: Held in reserve east of Little Round Top until

dark. As ordered, moved between the Round Tops collecting prisoners, arms, and caring for Federal wounded. Two men were wounded when fired on by possible friendly fire from Big Round Top. Led to the crest of the Big Round Top securing its position for the remainder of the battle.

Report of Colonel Joseph W. Fisher, Fifth Pennsylvania Reserves, HEADQUARTERS, THIRD BRIGADE, PENNSYLVANIA RESERVE CORPS, July 9, 1863.

SIR: Soon after the close of the fight of the 2d, I discovered in my immediate front a hill called Round Top, from the summit of which the enemy was doing us great damage. I thought it highly important that we should at once occupy it. I accordingly took two regiments of my brigade, viz, the Fifth, Lieutenant-Colonel Dare, and the Twelfth, Colonel Hardin, and the Twentieth Maine, commanded by Colonel Chamberlain, and at 10 p.m. ascended the hill, which was occupied by a full brigade of the enemy. We went up steadily in line of battle, taking over 30 prisoners in our ascent.

In the morning I discovered that the hill was of immense importance to us inasmuch as that if we had not taken it the enemy most undoubtedly would have done so, and in that event our left would have suffered very much, if, indeed, it could have held its position at all. I also discovered that our troops were not well posted for defense, so I changed my position, throwing the left flank of the two regiments which had not gone up the hill around so as to completely cover the ravine between the two hills, and at once threw up a stone wall across the entire ravine and up the hill, thus giving my men a sure protection against any advance which could possibly have been made by the enemy.

My officers and men behaved throughout with great coolness and bravery. Among others equally worthy of and deserving special mention, I beg leave to call your attention to the conduct of . . . Lieutenant-Colonel Dare, of the Fifth Regiment, who was also wounded at Fredericksburg, led his regiment up the hill, over rocks and ravines; . . . while all the subordinate field officers are deserving of special mention, especially Maj. James H. Larrimer, of the Fifth Regiment, who, suffering from acute rheumatism, refused to remain out of the battle.

My brigade captured and turned in to the proper

officer over 1,000 stand of arms, brought off over 200 wounded rebels, and buried 80 of their dead. Taking it all in all, I have no hesitation in saying that my brigade fulfilled their mission to Gettysburg.

UNIT: 6th Reserves. **OTHER NAME:** "35th Infantry."

ORGANIZATION: V Corps, 3rd Div., 1st Brig.

RAISED: From the counties of Bradford, Columbia, Dauphin, Franklin, Montour, Susquehanna, Tioga, & Wayne. **MUSTERED:** Camp Curtin, Harrisburg, no date.

COMMANDER: Lt. Col. Wellington H. Ent (1834-1871).

MONUMENT LOCATION: A beautiful 25' pillar, topped by a sphere, located along the Plum Run, 200 yards west of the Jacob Weikert house, approximately 100 yards north of the Wheatfield Road and east of the stone wall bordering the eastern edge of the Trostle Woods from the low marshy ground along the Plum Run. Represents their advanced position. One of the least visited monuments at Gettysburg. **MAP:** III, A-3.

STRENGTH: 10 Cos, 323 effectives. **LOSSES:** K-2, W-22, M-0. Total: 24. Percent Loss: 7.4.

WEAPONS: .58 Springfields.

SUMMARY: Advanced with the brigade from Cemetery Ridge, just north of Little Round Top, toward the Wheatfield, 700 yards away, moving west down the Wheatfield Road on the right of the brigade. Obliqued to the right (north) somewhere east of the present intersection of the Wheatfield Road, Crawford Ave., and Jacob Weikert farm lane. Passed through the left section of a Massachusetts battery, posted in the Weikert lane, that had been left on the field disabled. Redressed their ranks in the sunken farm lane, and as ordered, charged over a stonewall toward the Plum Run, 200 yards distant, continuing into the Trostle woods. A small detachment of volunteers from the right wing successfully charged the old Weikert home (today's house is post-battle, same foundation) and captured many enemy riflemen inside (see M.O.H. 6th Reserves). The charge to the Trostle woods was not severely contested as Wofford's Georgia Brigade was already disengaged and withdrawing back toward the Emmitsburg Road. The unit secured its position along Plum Run as indicated by their monument, leaving a strong skirmish line and returned east to the Weikert farm lane where it remained.

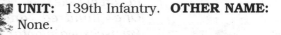

UNIT: 139th Infantry. **OTHER NAME:** None.

ORGANIZATION: VI Corps, 3rd Div., 3rd Brig.

RAISED: From the counties of Allegheny, Armstrong, and Mercer. **MUSTERED:** Camp Howell, Pittsburgh, Sept., 1, 1862.

COMMANDER: 1) Col. Frederick H. Coiller (1826-1906), accidentally wounded on July 3rd. 2) Lt. Col. William H. Moody (1834\35-1864), KIA at Cold Harbor.

MONUMENT LOCATION: On the Jacob Weikert farm, a few yards northeast of the intersection of the Wheatfield Road, Weikert farm lane, and Crawford Ave. The monument represents the position the regiment held after helping drive the enemy through the Trostle Woods. **MAP:** III, A-4 & IV, E-7.

STRENGTH: 10 Cos, 443 Effectives. **LOSSES:** K-1, W-19, M-0. Total: 20. Percent Loss: 4.5.

WEAPONS: .69 rifled Springfields.

SUMMARY: Advanced west from the ridge north of Little Round Top, in support of McCandless' Pennsylvania Reserves,

800 yards toward the Jacob Weikert Farm yard. The 139th's left flank mixed with the right of the 6th Reserves, as both regiments claimed possession of the left section of the 3rd Massachusetts battery posted above the farm lane. Supported a detachment of 6th Reserves who charged enemy riflemen holed up in the old Weikert house. Redressed their ranks in the farm lane and continued west on the right of the 6th Reserves, ending their charge at the Plum Run (somewhere near the present monument to the 6th). Many prisoners were captured, mostly too exhausted to continue their withdrawal. Returned to a position above Weikert's sunken lane, indicated by their present monument.

Report of Lieut. Col. William H. Moody, One hundred and thirty-ninth Pennsylvania Infantry. HDQRS. 139TH PENNSYLVANIA VOLUNTEERS, August 3, 1863.

SIR: About 5 o'clock in the evening the regiment, together with the rest of the brigade, was ordered into action on our left, which was seriously threatened. General Sykes' regulars, unable to withstand the fierce onslaught of the enemy, broke through our line in confusion. We delivered two volleys, and then charged on the enemy, driving him back in disorder. We lay that night and during the day of the 3d in the second line of battle, supporting the Pennsylvania Reserves.

Early on the morning of the 3d, Col. F. H. Collier accidentally shot himself through the foot with a pistol-ball, and was compelled to leave his command.

In the evening of the same day, the regiment took a prominent part in advancing our left, driving the enemy and recapturing one brass piece and three caissons belonging to the Ninth Massachusetts Battery.

UNIT: 93rd Infantry. **OTHER NAME:** None.

ORGANIZATION: VI Corps, 3rd Div., 3rd Brig.

RAISED: From the counties of Berks, Lebanon, & Montour. **MUSTERED:** Camp Coleman, Lebanon, Oct.

28, 1861.

COMMANDER: Maj. John I. Nevin (1819-1892).

MONUMENT LOCATIONS: 1) Twenty yards west of Sedgwick Ave., about 100 yards north of the Wheatfield Road. This monument represents the position before beginning its charge on July 2nd. Being that they were the center regiment in their brigade, one can get the general idea of the whole brigade as it stepped off. 2) In the Jacob Weikert farm yard, approximately 50 yards due south of the house, and 20 yards east of the farm lane, representing the position occupied after their charge, and which they held until the afternoon of July 3rd. **MAP:** III, A4/5.

STRENGTH: 10 Cos, 234 effectives. **LOSSES:** K-0, W-10, M-0. Total: 10. Percent Loss: 4.3.

WEAPONS: .69 rifled Springfields & .69 Smoothbores.

SUMMARY: Advanced west 800 yards from Cemetery Ridge, just north of Little Round Top, in support of McCandless' Pennsylvania Reserves, to the Jacob Weikert farm. Stopped along rail fence east of the farm yard to lend support to a detachment of 6th Pennsylvania Reserves as they voluntarily charged enemy riflemen in the old Weikert house. (Today's house is built on the old original foundation).

Resumed the charge unopposed toward the Plum Run collecting many prisoners. Returned to today's site of their 2nd monument in the Weikert farm yard for the night of July 2nd and all of July 3rd.

UNIT: 98th Infantry **OTHER NAME:** None.

ORGANIZATION: VI Corps, 3rd Div., 2nd Brig.

RAISED: Philadelphia.
MUSTERED: Camp Ballier, Philadelphia, Sept., 1862.

COMMANDER: Maj. John B. Kohler (1819-1864), KIA at Cedar Creek.

MONUMENT LOCATIONS: 1) About 50 yards west of Sykes Ave. on a rocky shelf on the north shoulder of Little Round Top. Represents the regiment's first position on the afternoon of July 2nd when it formed in line of battle prior to its charge into the Valley of Death. 2) see July 3rd.
MAP: III, B-5.

STRENGTH: 10 Cos, 351 effectives. **LOSSES:** K-0, W-11, M-0. Total: 11. Percent Loss: .03.

WEAPONS: .58 Springfields & French rifles.

SUMMARY: Separated from its brigade by retreating U.S. regulars, the 98th along with the 121st New York on its left formed a demi-brigade in line of battle on today's Sykes Ave., on Little Round Top. Moved to support the Pennsylvania Reserves who were deploying for a charge toward the Wheatfield, 700 yards to the west. Prior to the reservists' charge and before ordered, Maj. Kohler advanced the 98th with a loud cheer, bounding over the crest toward the Plum Run valley below. Col. Upton of the 121st, who had not yet received orders to charge, watched astonished as the 98th obliqued at left angles across his front from right to left, and through an equally astonished gun crew from a section of 12-pounders from an Ohio battery, immediately ceased fire. Moving into the Valley of Death with bayonets fixed, the 98th charged down the rocky west slope toward the Valley of Death, meeting little resistance as they became entangled with U.S. regulars retreating eastward. The 98th's attack stalled at the muddy run, the men forming a firing line in knee-deep muck just east of today's Crawford Ave., approximately 300 yards south of the Wheatfield Road. As ordered, advanced with McCandless' Pennsylvania Reserve Brigade as they carried the Wheatfield and north Houck's

July 2nd

Ridge. The 98th advanced into the Rose Woods driving the few remaining enemy away from the stone wall on the crest. Secured their position until 10:00 p.m., when ordered to the right, toward the Jacob Weikert farm. Went into position near the Weikert farm house, as indicated by their No. 2 monument where they remained until July 5th.

Report of Maj. John B. Kohler, Ninety-eighth Pennsylvania Infantry. HDQRS. NINETY-EIGHTH REGT. PENNSYLVANIA VOLS., August 1, 1863.

SIR: On July 1, about 9 p.m., the regiment started from near Manchester, Md., where it had been resting since the previous evening, marched all night, and the following day arrived in the vicinity of the battle-field, to the left of Gettysburg, about 3 p. m., where soon after it formed in line of battle, supporting the part of the Second Corps which was engaged with the enemy. While getting into position, the regiment lost 1 officer and 9 men wounded by the enemy's sharpshooters. During the whole of the 3d, the regiment was lying in the front line of battle, exposed to the enemy's fire, but protected by a stone wall. Here Lieutenant Manthe, of Company A, was wounded by one of the enemy's sharpshooters.

UNIT: 95th Infantry. **OTHER NAME:** "45 or 54th Volunteers," "Gosline's Zouaves."

ORGANIZATION: VI Corps, 1st Div., 2nd Brig.

RAISED: Philadelphia.
MUSTERED: Camp Gibson, Philadelphia, Oct. 18, 1862.

COMMANDER: Lt. Col. Edward C. Carroll (1825-1864), KIA at the Wilderness.

MONUMENT LOCATION: On the north shoulder of the Wheatfield Road, approximately 100 yards east of the Plum Run. Represents the most advanced position. **MAP III.**

STRENGTH: 10 Cos, 309 effectives. **LOSSES:** K-0, W-2, M-0. Total: 2. Percent Loss: .1.

WEAPONS: .58 Springfields.

SUMMARY: Advanced in line of battle 200 yards in rear of McCandless' Pennsylvania Reserves (following the 11th Reserves) from the ridge north of Little Round Top, west toward the Wheatfield. Moved toward the Plum Run, their right flank very near the Wheatfield Road. Light engagement as the Reserves in their front were forced back, taking most of the resistance to the west. Pulled back to a rail fence at the site of their present monument, going into a reserve position for the remainder of the battle. Held this position until July 5th.

UNIT: 96th Infantry.
OTHER NAME: None.

ORGANIZATION: VI Corps, 1st Div., 3rd Brig.

RAISED: Schuylkill County. **MUSTERED:** Lawton Hill, Pottsville, Sept., 23 1861.

COMMANDER: Maj. William H. Lessig (1831-1910).

MONUMENT LOCATION: On the north shoulder of the Wheatfield Road, approximately 40 yards east of the Jacob Weikert farm lane in the Valley of Death. The monument represents the advanced position. **MAP:** III, A-4.

STRENGTH: 10 Cos, 309 effectives. **LOSSES:** K-0, W-1, M-0. Total: 1. Percent Loss: .003.

WEAPONS: .58 Springfields & .577 Enfields.

SUMMARY: Advanced in line of battle 200 yards in rear of McCandless' Pennsylvania Reserves, following the 6th Reserves from the ridge north of Little Round Top toward the Jacob Weikert farm, a distance of about 800 yards. Engagement was light as the Reserves had forced back most of the Confederate resistance. Pulled back east of the Weikert farm yard and went into reserve position behind a stone and rail fence at the site of their present monument. Held this position until July 5th.

UNIT: 9th Reserves. **OTHER NAME:** "38th Infantry."

ORGANIZATION: V Corps, 3rd Div., 3rd Brig.

RAISED: From the counties of Allegheny, Beaver & Crawford. **MUSTERED:** Camp Curtin, Harrisburg. July 27, 1861.

COMMANDER: Lt. Col. James M. Snodgrass (1806-1883).

MONUMENT LOCATION: Below the southern-most tip of Little Round Top just northwest of the Warren and Sykes Avenues intersection in the saddle between the Round Tops. Represents the position held for the remainder of the battle. **MAP:** III, D-5.

STRENGTH: 10 Cos, 320 effectives. **LOSSES:** K-0, W-5, M-0. Total: 5. Percent Loss: 1.6.

WEAPONS: .69 Smoothbores.

SUMMARY: Not actively engaged in battle. Moved up from a reserve position in rear of Little Round Top. Attended to Federal wounded and collected prisoners. Five men wounded when two companies were sent toward the Plum Run, 400 yards due west of present day monument, to establish a skirmish line. (Very possibly hit by friendly fire in the dark).

UNIT: 10th Reserves. **OTHER NAME:** "39th Infantry."

ORGANIZATION: V Corps, 3rd Div., 3rd Brig.

RAISED: From the counties of Beaver, Clarion, Crawford, Mercer, Somerset, Venango, Warren & Washington. **MUSTERED:** Camp Wright, Pittsburgh. July 21, 1861.

COMMANDER: Col. Adoniram J. Warner (1834-1910).

MONUMENT LOCATION: In the saddle between the Round Tops, 100 yards due south of the interesection of Warren & Sykes Avenues. Represents the exact position held by the regiment. **MAP:** III, D-6.

STRENGTH: 10 Cos, 401 effectives. **LOSSES:** K-2, W-3, M-0. Total: 5. Percent Loss: 1.2.

WEAPONS: .577 Enfields.

SUMMARY: Not actively engaged. Held in reserve in rear of Little Round Top. Secured their position behind the stone wall running parallel to Sykes Ave. (the stone wall continued north past Warren Avenue at the time of the battle), their right flank reaching the 9th Reserves' left flank, located below Little Round Top. Several companies were sent forward toward Plum Run as skirmishers. Two men were shot and killed with three wounded during this action, either picked off by enemy sharpshooters or shot by friendly fire in the dark. Remained in this position for the rest of the battle.

UNIT: 119th Infantry. **OTHER NAME:** "Gray's Reserves."

ORGANIZATION: VI Corps, 1st Div. 3rd Brig.

RAISED: From the County of Philadelphia. **MUSTERED:** Camp Halleck, Philadelphia. Sept. 1,1862.

COMMANDER: Col. Peter C. Ellmaker (1813-1890).

MONUMENT LOCATION: 1) Located in rear (east) of the Round Tops on Howe Ave., about 50 yards east of the Taneytown Road. **MAP:** III, G-8 & F-5.

STRENGTH: 10 Cos, 466 effectives. **LOSSES:** K-0, W-2, M-0. Total: 2. Percent Lost: .5.

WEAPONS: .58 Springfields.

SUMMARY: Arrived with the brigade in the afternoon and took position in the field east of the Taneytown Road, (Howe Ave.) their own right flank resting near the Taneytown Road. As ordered, marched one-half mile north to the present intersection of the Wheatfield and Taneytown Roads, going into a line of battle just west of the intersection. (No marker) Returned south to position indicated by present monument. 2) Big Round Top, representing their position on July 3rd.

UNIT: 68th Infantry. **OTHER NAME:** "Scott Legion."

ORGANIZATION: III Corps, 1st Div., 1st Brig.

RAISED: From the counties of Montgomery & Philadelphia. **MUSTERED:** Camp Frankford, Philadelphia, Sept. 2, 1862.

COMMANDER: 1) Col. Andrew H. Tippin (1822-1870), assumed command of 1st Brig on Gen. Graham's wounding. 2) Capt. Milton S. Davis (1824-1863), K.I.A. Mine Run Campaign.

MONUMENT LOCATIONS: 1) Center of the artillery line in the Sherfy Peach Orchard along the Wheatfield Road.

Monument represents four positions occupied at different locations, all within eyesight of this marker. 2) This monument, located in the Peach Orchard along the Emmitsburg Road, represents the regiment's forward southern-most position during the battle. **MAP:** IV, F-5 & I-2..

STRENGTH: 10 Cos, 320 effectives. **LOSSES:** K-13, W-126, M-13. Total: 152 Percent: 47.5.

WEAPONS: .577 Enfields.

SUMMARY: Advanced with brigade into the oat field in rear of the Sherfy Peach Orchard, approximately 200 yards due north of their present No. 1 monument, in support of a New Jersey battery along the Wheatfield Road indicated by No. 2. Advanced due south into the Peach Orchard south of the Wheatfield Road, changed direction and moved west toward the Emmitsburg Road. Helped in slowing Kershaw's first assault and Semmes' attack, but was soundly beaten when Barksdale's Mississippians hit them on the right flank. Forced back, the regiment faced about to the west, from atop the rise in the Peach Orchard, about 200 yards west-northwest of their No. 1 monument. Faced about under extreme pressure and attempted to form a firing line. Flanked on the right by overpowering numbers, the 68th retreated in some disorder back to Cemetery Ridge.

Report of Col. Andrew H. Tippin, Sixty-eighth Pennsylvania Infantry. HDQRs. SIXTY-EIGHTH REGT. PENNSYLVANIA VOLS., August 4, 1863.

LIEUTENANT: On the morning of July 2, I moved my regiment with the brigade to the position assigned us in a large open field in the rear of our line of skirmishers, then engaged with the enemy's skirmishers in front. The brigade was deployed in line of battle by battalions, doubled on the center, my regiment being on the left of the line.

After remaining in this position some time, the brigade was moved farther to the front, immediately in rear of Clark's battery, deployed in line of battle, and ordered to lie down. We remained in this position nearly two hours, suffering severely from the destructive fire of the enemy's batteries posted on our left and front. I was then ordered to move my regiment forward into a peach orchard, and fronting a road running parallel with the enemy's front. We had been in this position but a short time when significant movements on the part of the enemy made it evident we were about to be attacked. Soon he advanced. I ordered the men

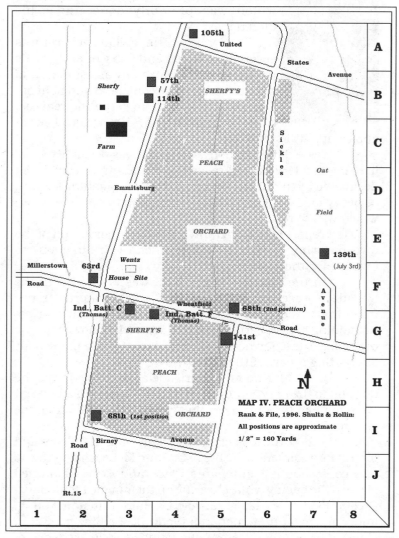

MAP IV. PEACH ORCHARD

Rank & File, 1996. Shultz & Rollins

All positions are approximate

1/2" = 160 Yards

to reserve their fire until reaching a certain point, when a destructive fire was opened, the enemy halting and dropping behind a fence. Receiving re-enforcements, and heavy masses of his infantry coming down on our right, I ordered

my command to fall back to the position in the rear of the batteries, which was done in good order. Here I met General Graham, who ordered me at once to engage the enemy coming down on our right flank, which was promptly done under his directions.

Here, too, the gallant general was severely wounded and subsequently made prisoner. He declined any assistance, and directed me to take command and fight on. I supposed him able to get to the rear, as, after dismounting, he walked with apparently little difficulty.

We held the position as long as it was possible to hold it. The artillery having retired, and the ranks very much decimated by the fire of the enemy, who was pushing forward in heavy masses, I ordered the command to retire in order, which was done

I reported to General Ward, now in command of the division, who assigned me a position, with directions to bivouac for the night.

On the morning of the 3d, I was ordered with the brigade to proceed with the division to a field a short distance from the place where we bivouacked, and stack arms. Remaining but a short time, I was ordered to move with the division to the left, where we formed line of battle in the rear, supporting a part of the Fifth Army Corps.

In the afternoon, the brigade again moved with the division to the rear of the center and in support of a battery. We remained here until evening, when I was relieved of the command.

I regret the loss of a great many gallant officers and men of my regiment. The brave Captain McLearn and the no less conspicuous Lieutenants Black and Reynolds all fell close to the enemy while cheering on their men. Lieutenant-Colonel Reynolds, Major Winslow, Captains Funston, Young, and Fulmer, and Lieutenants [John J.] Fenlin, jr., Ealer, Guest, Porter, and Heston, all wounded, bear evidence of their good conduct and gallant behavior. I can also bear testimony to the gallantry of the other officers of the command.

Of the non-commissioned officers and privates of the regiment I cannot speak with too much praise. Their obedience to command and the determined stand made against overwhelming odds, their thinned ranks fully prove. Animated by the glorious cause in which they were engaged, each vied with the other in deeds of gallant daring.

UNIT: 63rd Infantry. **OTHER NAME:** None.

ORGANIZATION: III Corps, 1st Div., 1st Brig.

RAISED: From the counties of Allegheny & Clarion. **MUSTERED:** Camp Haus, Washington D.C., Oct. 1861.

COMMANDER: Maj. John A. Danks (1626-1896).

MONUMENT LOCATION: Approximately 300 yards due south of the Sherfy farm house, on the northwest corner of the intersection of the Emmitsburg, Millerstown, and Wheatfield Roads. **MAP:** IV, F-2.

STRENGTH: 10 cos, 246 effectives. **LOSSES:** K-1, W-29, M-4, Total: 34. Percent Loss: 13.8.

WEAPONS: .54 & .577 Austrians.

SUMMARY: Deployed on picket duty early in the morning, approximately 300 yards west of the present monument on the Emmitsburg Road, dissecting today's Millerstown Road. Engaged throughout the afternoon with enemy sharpshooters and advanced skirmishers. Pulled back on the the initial advance of Longstreet's attack. Withdrew back to Cemetery Ridge. Not engaged during the main battle of July 2nd. Held in reserve in rear of McGilvery's artillery line throughout the morning and great cannonade of July 3rd. Moved forward on Pickett's advance, some of its men squeezing into the vacated position of Thompson's Ind. Battery and engaging Kemper's line as it moved north. Most of the regiment held its position at the site of the present Pennsylvania monument, exposed to severe artillery fire. Pickets were sent forward to the Plum Run. Held this position until midnight when they were moved into the position occupied by the Vermont Brigade, relieving them of their works. Held this position for the remainder of the battle. Helped bury the dead.

Report of Maj. John A. Danks, Sixty-third Pennsylvania Infantry. HDQRs. SIXTY-THIRD PENNSYLVANIA VOLUNTEERS. July 10, 1863.

LIEUTENANT: On the morning of July 2, the enemy made his appearance in our front, and opened fire on our outposts. Firing was kept up until the general engagement was brought on, between the hours of 3 and 4 p. m.

At 5.30 p. m. the regiment was relieved from the picket line by a regiment of the Second Division, Third Corps. I then withdrew the regiment, our ammunition having been exhausted; fell back in good order, when I met the balance of the brigade, and, after a few minutes' rest, moved forward with the brigade to an open field, where we encamped for the night.

Early on the morning of the 3d, we were again ordered to the front, where we lay in position until 10 a. m., when the enemy attempted to pierce the center of the line. To this point we were ordered to move as rapidly as possible, which the regiment accomplished, and immediately took a position in support of a battery. We were exposed during the day to a severe fire of shot and shell.

UNIT: 141st Infantry. **OTHER NAME:** None.

ORGANIZATION: III Corps. 1st Div., 1st Brig.

RAISED: From the counties of Bradford, Susquehanna, and Wayne. **MUSTERED:** Camp Curtin, Harrisburg, August 1862.

COMMANDER: Col. Henry J. Mandill (1829-1899).

MONUMENT LOCATION: Atop the small knoll in the

northeast corner of the Sherfy Peach Orchard that commands the intersection of the Wheatfield Road (Fairfield Crossroad) and Birney Ave. **MAP** IV, G-5..

STRENGTH: 10 Cos, 209 effectives. **LOSSES:** K-25, W-103, M-21. Total: 149. Percent Loss: 71.3.

WEAPONS: .58 Springfields & .54 Austrians.

SUMMARY: Advanced into an oat field in rear of the Sherfy Peach Orchard near 2:00 p.m in support of a New Jersey Battery. Laid in rear of battery, facing due south, for over an hour, taking incoming artillery. Advanced as ordered across the Wheatfield Road and into the southern portion of the Peach Orchard, taking heavy casualties from enfilading enemy artillery fire from the west. Ordered to advance south to the edge of the Peach Orchard, approximately 200 yards south of present monument, and engaged Kershaw's attacking lines as they crossed the Emmitsburg Road near the Rose Farm. Withdrew as Confederate reinforcements swept across the road taking them on the right flank. Pulled back to the Wentz house and helped to temporarily check Barksdale's advance while allowing several Federal batteries the time needed to pull off the crossroad, taking horrible casualties. Routed in disorder, retreated north-northeast to Cemetery Ridge.

Report of Col. Henry J. Madill, One hundred and forty-first Pennsylvania Infantry. Hdqrs. 141st Regiment Pennsylvania Volunteers, __, __, 1863
    SIR: During the forenoon of July 2, we moved into a field beyond a small house and to the left of a road leading from the wooden house, near which General Sickles established his headquarters, to the Emmitsburg pike, and here, by command of General Graham, we then formed in line of battle, the Fifty-seventh Pennsylvania Volunteers on the right of the line, the Sixty-eighth Pennsylvania Volunteers on the left, and my regiment in the center, the One hundred and fifth and One hundred and fourteenth Pennsylvania Volunteers supporting.
    The line was doubled on the center, Clark's battery in our front. They delivered a few shots, receiving but little response. The battery then moved up the hill and a little to

the left, and took a position in the peach orchard, near the Emmitsburg pike. In the meanwhile our line advanced up the slope and deployed in the oat-field, some 15 rods from the pike, and were ordered to lie down. At this point we sustained a severe fire from artillery for some time, the enemy having a good range.

After remaining in this position for some twenty minutes or more, I received an order from General Graham, through the acting assistant adjutant-general (Lieutenant [Charles H.] Graves), to move my regiment out, and place it in front of Clark's battery. This order was in a few minutes countermanded, and I formed my regiment in rear of that battery, and, while supporting that battery, the Second New Hampshire was ordered up to my support. They took position in my rear. Here the fire from the enemy's artillery was very severe, and we sustained a considerable loss in killed and wounded.

At this time it was observed that the enemy was advancing in strong force from across and down the Emmitsburg pike. My regiment, together with two others (the Third Michigan [Colonel Pierce], and Third Maine, Colonel Lakeman), were ordered to the front of the peach orchard, the battery occupying that position having withdrawn and left the field. We advanced, the Third Maine on my right and the Third Michigan (Colonel Pierce) on my left.

The enemy was advancing in two columns, one column crossing the pike beyond the stone barn and advancing in two lines in the direction of the position occupied by the Second and Third Brigades, which were to our left and somewhat to our rear. When they advanced below the stone barn, they endeavored to extend their lines to the left. It was at this time that my regiment, with the two others spoken of, was ordered forward. We engaged the flank of the enemy, and prevented him from extending his lines this side of the small creek that runs through the field near the stone barn.

At this time the other column had advanced up to the pike and deployed, and was marching on the point we were occupying. The battery in position near the road and immediately to the left of the log house withdrew. The Third Maine, after exchanging a few shots with the enemy at this point, withdrew. Colonel Pierce's regiment (Third Michigan) withdrew about the same time, or a few minutes before. I found myself alone, with a small regiment of about 180 men.

I continued to hold my position for a short time, when I withdrew from that position and took a position in rear of the Sixty-eighth Pennsylvania Volunteers, who were engaged with the enemy in front of the barn, near the brick house. When I took this position the Sixty-eighth withdrew, the balance of the brigade having previously withdrawn. I was thus left alone on the hill occupied by the brigade in the afternoon. The enemy, after the falling back of the Sixty-eighth, advanced to the barn. I engaged them at this point, and held them in check for twenty minutes or upward, but being overpowered by the large numbers of the enemy, I was compelled to retire, which I reluctantly did.

It was at this point that my regiment suffered so severely; 25 of my men were killed here and 5 of my officers severely wounded, besides a large number of non-commissioned officers. Among the severely wounded, and who have since died, were the color-bearers and all of the color guard.

I would especially call attention to Sergt. Maj. Joseph G. Fell for his good conduct on the field. The part he took in fearlessly exposing himself during the whole of the fight, and especially during the latter part of it, deserves to be particularly noticed; also Corporal Berry, who carried the colors. Though wounded three times, he refused to give up his colors, and did not yield them until helplessly stricken down the fourth time. Such men deserve particular notice.

Of the conduct of my officers and men, I am happy to say that they are all entitled to great credit. Not one of my men failed me under the most trying circumstances, and to my officers I am under great obligations for their coolness and efficiency under the circumstances.

I regret to say that Major Spalding received two severe wounds, one in each leg, and that he was taken prisoner by the enemy. He lost his left leg; it was amputated below the knee by the enemy.

UNIT: Independent Batteries C & F consolidated.
OTHER NAME: "Thompson's."

ORGANIZATION: 1st Volunteer Reserve Artillery Brigade.

RAISED: Allegheny County. **MUSTERED:** Battery C, Pittsburgh, Oct. 1861. Battery F, Camp Lamon, Williamsport, Maryland, Nov. 1861. Consolidated on June, 3, 1863.

COMMANDER: Capt. James Thompson (1821-1906).

MONUMENT'S & LOCATION: 1) Battery C: On south side of the Wheatfield Road in the Sherfy Peach Orchard, approximately 75 yards east of the Emmitsburg Road. 2) Battery F: A few yards north of battery C's monument. Both markers represent the approximate position of two sections from Thompson's battery, the third being in the Sherfy farmyard west of the Emmitsburg Road. **MAP** IV, F-3/4.

STRENGTH: 2 Cos, 105 Effectives. **LOSSES:** K-2, W-23, M-3. Total: 28. Percent Loss: 26.7.

WEAPONS: Six 3-inch Ordnance Rifles.

SUMMARY: Two sections went into position in the Sherfy Peach Orchard near the present monuments, south of the Wheatfield Road, facing due south, with one section going into position near the Sherfy Barn, facing due west, west of the Emmitsburg Road. Held position in the Peach Orchard until nearly overrun, pulling back north of the Wheatfield Road and into an oat field about 200 yards north of the monuments. The rise to the west helped conceal these guns from Barksdale's troops along the Emmitsburg Road. All four rifles limbered to the rear, the last being done with only two wheel horses, a determined driver, and Thompson tugging at a bridle. (See Pvt. Casper Carlisle, Co F. M.O.H.)

The section in the Sherfy farmyard was overrun, then recaptured by a desperate countercharge by a Pennsylvania regiment, allowing the gunners the time needed to pull back safely. All six cannons retreated back to an impromptu artillery line being formed 1200 yards northeast of the monuments. Five cannons engaged Barksdale's Mississippians as they crossed their front heading northeast toward Plum Run. Point blank canister at right enfilade helped to check their advance.

UNIT: 57th (Co's D & G disbanded). **OTHER NAME:** None.

ORGANIZATION: II Corps. 1st Div., 1st Brig.

RAISED: From the counties of Bradford, Crawford, Mercer, & Tioga. **MUSTERED:** Camp Curtin, Harrisburg, Oct. 14, 1861.

COMMANDER: 1) Col. Peter Sides (1820-1878), wounded in action. 2) Capt. Alanson H. Nelson (1828-1921).

MONUMENT LOCATION: Enclosed within a small iron fence, the monument is located just north of the Sherfy Barn and west of the Emmitsburg Road. Monument represents the regiment's position as it accepted Barksdale's frontal and flank attack. **MAP:** IV, B-3.

STRENGTH: 8 Cos, 207 Effectives. **LOSSES:** K-11, W-46, M-58. Total: 115, Percent Loss: 55.6.

WEAPONS: .577 Enfields & .54 Austrians.

SUMMARY: Advanced to the western edge of the Sherfy farm yard (150 ft. west of present day monument) where it met the attack of Barksdale's Mississippi Brigade, while under a terrible artillery fire. Held its ground in vicious hand-to-hand combat, allowing a section of Thompson's Pennsylvania battery the time needed to prolonge back before limbering. Outflanked and outnumbered, the regiment fell back east of the Emmitsburg Road in disorder, retreating to Cemetery Ridge. Held in reserve in rear of McGilvery's line throughout the morning of July 3rd. Moved forward in support of Doubleday's line during Pickett's Charge. Some men possibly engaged. Most of the regiment were unengaged and were sent forward on Pickett's repulse to collect prisoners and form a picket line in the Plum Run. About midnight the 57th moved forward to relieve Stannard's Vermont Brigade. Held this position for the remainder of the battle.

Report of Capt. Alanson H. Nelson, Fifty-seventh Pennsylvania Infantry, First Brigade.

CAMP IN THE FIELD, July 10, 1863.

SIR: The next morning [July 2] we advanced to the right and rear of the peach orchard, and remained about one hour; then advanced to the front and deployed, taking a position on the right of the one hundred and fourteenth Pennsylvania Volunteers and near the brick house, where we were exposed to a very severe shelling for about two hours, when, at the request of Captain Randolph, we advanced to the brick house and met the enemy in force, who was advancing on us in three lines.

We engaged him about twenty minutes. but, being overpowered by a superior force, we were obliged to fall back, the One hundred and fourteenth Pennsylvania Volunteers having done so already. We finally reformed in the rear, near the Baltimore pike and a large yellow barn, where we remained until 8 a. m. of the next day (3d instant), when we were ordered to the front as a reserve. About 3 P. M. on the 3d instant, we were ordered forward with the brigade to support a battery in General Doubleday's division, First Corps, where we remained until dark; then moved to the front, and acted as a picket reserve until the morning of the 4th instant, when we moved to the left and in rear of a line of breastworks, where we remained until ordered on the present march. All in the command acted well and fought bravely, and where all acted so well it was impossible for one to distinguish himself more than another.

UNIT: 105th. **OTHER NAME:** "Wild Cat Regiment."

ORGANIZATION: III Corps, 1st Div., 1st Brig.

RAISED: From the counties of Allegheny, Jefferson, & Westmoreland. **MUSTERED:** Camp Wilkens, Pittsburgh. Sept. 9, 1861.

COMMANDER: Col. Calvin A. Craig (1833-1864).

MONUMENT LOCATION: Northeast corner at the intersection of the Emmitsburg Rd. and U.S. Ave. (Trostle Ln.) Monument represents the second battle position occupied by the regiment. **MAP:** IV, A-4.

STRENGTH: 10 Cos, 259 Effectives. **LOSSES:** K-8, W-115, M-9. Total: 132. Percent Loss; 48.2.

WEAPONS: .58 Springfields.

SUMMARY FOR JULY 2ND: Initial battle line was west of the Emmitsburg Road, facing west, with the left flank near the Sherfy barn, the right flank across from the Trostle farm lane (U. S. Ave.) intersection (50 yards west of present day monument). Severely hit by artillery fire and infantry sharpshooters, taking many casualties. Accepted Longstreet's attack until flanked on the left. Pulled back to the Trostle farm lane, changing direction to face south and meet new threat. Held the rail fence on the north side of the Trostle farm lane as indicated by monument, until forced back by Barksdale's advancing Mississippians. Retreated slowly to the northeast toward Cemetery Ridge, facing about to check pursuing enemy. Rallied in support of II Corps reinforcements. Laid in reserve in rear of McGilvery's artillery line throughout the morning and great cannonade of July 3rd. Moved forward in support of the artillery, some men engaged at the position once occupied by Thompson's battery. Held their position near today's Pennsylvania monument until midnight when they were sent forward to relieve Stannard's Vermont Brigade. Details were sent to help bury the dead.

Report of Col. Calvin A. Craig, One hundred and fifth Pennsylvania Infantry. HEADQUARTERS 1O5TH PENNSYLVANIA VOLUNTEERS, July 11, 1863.

LIEUTENANT: On the morning of the 2d, we moved with the balance of the brigade a short distance, when line of battle was formed about half a mile east of and parallel with the Emmitsburg road, in which position we remained until 11.15 a. m., when we received orders to move to the front to support the Sixty-third Pennsylvania Volunteers, who were deployed as skirmishers along the Emmitsburg road. My regiment took position immediately in their rear, with Companies A, F, D, I, and C deployed, the other companies in reserve. The fire from the enemy's sharpshooters was severe. One man was killed very soon after we got into position.

At 1 p. m. orders were received from General Graham to rejoin the brigade, and to take position in rear of the Fifty-seventh Pennsylvania Volunteers, and on the right of the One hundred and fourteenth Pennsylvania Volunteers, in column doubled on the center

The regiment remained in this position until 2 p. m. We then moved forward with the brigade to a point near the brick house on the Emmitsburg road, where we halted and deployed, still maintaining our relative positions, my right resting on a by-road running at right angles with the Emmitsburg road. At this time the enemy opened with his artillery a very destructive fire. My regiment suffered a loss of some 12 men while in this position.

At 4 p. m. we again moved forward near the brick house and immediately in its rear. At this time I noticed the enemy's infantry advancing from the woods on the left of the house and in its rear, and seeing that I could do nothing in the position I then occupied (in the rear of the Fifty-seventh Pennsylvania Volunteers), and that I must necessarily suffer severely, I ordered the regiment forward to fill a vacancy on the right of the Fifty-seventh Pennsylvania Volunteers, in the front line and a little beyond the Emmitsburg road. Having gained this position, the fire from the enemy being very severe, we immediately opened fire.

After occupying this position for a short time, I noticed the regiments on my immediate left (One hundred and fourteenth and Fifty-seventh Pennsylvania Volunteers) cluster in groups behind the brick house and adjacent out-buildings. A few moments later the One hundred and fourteenth fell to the rear, and the Fifty-seventh very soon followed, leaving my left flank entirely unprotected.

The enemy, taking advantage of this, advanced across the Emmitsburg road, in front of the house, and immediately opened fire upon our Left flank. Seeing this, I ordered my regiment to retire slowly a short distance, and changed front to the rear on the first company. A small remnant of the Fifty-seventh Pennsylvania Volunteers rallied with us, and formed line along the by-road before mentioned, where we again opened fire, and checked the advancing rebels for a few minutes; but the regiment being so small and both flanks being entirely unprotected, I ordered the regiment to retire slowly, and formed line again a short distance to the rear. The troops in our rear by this time were beginning to be effective, and the brigade having gone to the rear, I formed with these troops, and fought with them, sometimes advancing and sometimes retreating, but do not know whose troops they were.

Soon after, I saw General Humphreys, and formed line with some of his troops. From this point we advanced steadily until we had regained nearly all the ground we had lost. Noticing at this time three pieces of artillery that had been abandoned by our artillerists and turned upon us by the advancing rebels (and who were in turn compelled to abandon them), I sent forward my few remaining men to bring them off the field, but being unable to bring them all off, I got assistance from some men of the Excelsior Brigade with two of the pieces, and brought the third off the field with my own men. I withdrew all my men with this piece, and finally delivered it to Sergt. Daniel A. Whitesell, Battery C, Fifth U. S. Artillery, who identified it as one of the pieces belonging to that battery.

The next morning, July 3, we again moved forward with the brigade, and occupied a position in the third line of battle and in the rear of the Fifth Corps, where we remained until about 2 p. m., when we were again ordered with the brigade to the center, our forces there having been attacked, and formed line of battle in the rear of the batteries at that point. We remained in this position until 9 p. m., when the regiment with the brigade moved to the front and formed line of battle on the first line, relieving the Vermont Brigade, of the First Corps. We remained in this position during the night.

The regiment never fought better or with more enthusiasm. No instance of cowardice occurred during the engagements. All seemed to feel that they were fighting on the soil of their native State, and that they would either conquer or yield up their lives in her defense.

I cannot make particular mention of individual bravery. All, both officers and men, seemed imbued with the same spirit, which was one of determination never to yield, but to fight to the bitter end, and until there was not a single rebel in arms to pollute the soil of their native State.

UNIT: 114th Infantry. **OTHER NAME:** "Collis' Zouaves."

ORGANIZATION: III Corps, 1st Div., 3rd Brig.

RAISED: Philadelphia. **MUSTERED:** Camp Banks, Philadelphia (Germantown) Sept. 1, 1862.

COMMANDER: 1) Lt. Col. Frederick F. Cavada (1832-1871), captured on July 2nd. 2) Capt. Edward R. Bowan (1839-1908).

MONUMENT LOCATION: Beautiful bronze statue of a Zouave soldier atop a large granite pedestal surrounded by a black iron fence, located on the west shoulder of the Emmitsburg Road at the Sherfy farmyard. Represents the position occupied by the regiment during Barksdale's advance. **MAP:** IV, B-3.

STRENGTH: 10 Cos, 259 effectives. **LOSSES:** K-9, W-86, M-60. Total: 149. Percent Loss: 59.8.

WEAPONS: .58 Springfields & .577 Enfields.

SUMMARY: Advanced into an oat field in rear of the Sherfy Peach Orchard sometime near 2:00 P.M., facing due south in rear of the rise east of the Emmitsburg Road. Supported a New Jersey battery engaging along the Wheatfield Road a few yards to their front. Changed direction to the west (right) and advanced to the Emmitsburg Road as a New Hampshire battery pulled out near the Sherfy farmyard. Split into two wings, the regiment was pummeled by Barksdale's overpowering numbers from the left, front and right. Held its ground along the Emmitsburg Road until massive casualties and confusion it unreasonable to continue the fight. Swept away in total disorder retreating to the north-northeast through the Trostle farm and on to Cemetery Ridge. Held in reserve in rear of McGilvery's artillery line throughout July 3rd. (see citation for July 3rd.

Report of Capt. Edward R. Bowen, One hundred and fourteenth Pennsylvania Infantry. Fox's GAP, SOUTH MOUNTAIN,

MD., July 12, 1863.

SIR: The regiment moved to the front on the morning of the 2d, and at 1 p. m. advanced to the front of the woods and formed with the brigade a line of battle, in columns doubled on the center, to the left and rear of the Fifty-seventh Pennsylvania Volunteers.

Clark's (First New Jersey) battery then took up a position in front, and opened on the enemy. We remained here until ordered to advance with the brigade, maintaining the same position to the Fifty-seventh Pennsylvania Volunteers until we reached an oat-field, where we were ordered to deploy, which we did, the One hundred and fifth Pennsylvania Volunteers being on our right and the Sixty-eighth Pennsylvania Volunteers on our left. At this moment we were ordered to lie down. The enemy then opened on us with his batteries, and for about two and a half hours we lay under a most severe fire, losing, however, but few men, the enemy's range being too high.

Captain Randolph, chief of artillery of the corps, at this moment rode up to the regiment, and ordered us to advance, saying, "If you want to save my battery, move forward. I cannot find the General. I give the order on my own responsibility." We then advanced, passing through his battery, which immediately limbered up and went to the rear, and the regiment, crossing the road, formed a line of battle, our line on the right joining the Fifty-seventh Pennsylvania Volunteers.

Seeing the enemy advancing in force, I ordered the right wing of the regiment to advance to the rear of the brick house, and attempted to form a line with the Fifty-seventh Pennsylvania Volunteers, who were already there. In this I was but partially successful, as the enemy had already advanced so quickly and in such force as to gain the road, and, pouring a murderous fire on our flank, threw the left wing of the regiment on to the right in much confusion. I attempted to rally the regiment across the road, but could not succeed in doing so, the enemy advancing so rapidly and my men falling in such numbers as to prevent my succeeding in doing so. I succeeded, however, in rallying a number around the colors, and brought them off, but, in doing so, got separated from the brigade, and night coming on, I was unable to find them, although I used every effort to do so.

I remained where I was until early daylight of the 3d,

when I rejoined the brigade, and we lay all the morning of the 3d in the woods, where we were supplied with rations, and remained until about 3 p. m., when I was ordered to move up to the right by the double-quick, being detached from the brigade to support Cowan's (First New York) battery.

At this time, Colonel Madill, of the One hundred and forty-first Pennsylvania Volunteers, assumed command of the brigade, and I took command of his regiment and my own.

At about 7 p. m. I was ordered to get ready to be relieved, and to send to the front a detail to collect the arms which had been left there. We collected about 300 pieces.

While falling back from the brick house on to the road, and very hotly pressed by the enemy, I saw Lieutenant-Colonel Cavada, who was then commanding the regiment, stopping at a log house in an orchard on our right. I inquired if he was wounded; he replied that he was not, but utterly exhausted. I begged him to make an effort to come on, as the enemy were only a few yards from him and advancing rapidly. He replied that he could not, and I left him there, and not having heard from him since, I have no doubt he was taken prisoner there. I assumed command of the regiment at this time.

I also report a number of men as missing whom I have no doubt were killed and their bodies burned when the barn was burned down, and some, I have no doubt, were taken prisoners at the brick house, among them 2 second lieutenants.

In closing this report, I beg leave to ask that it may be remembered that I was not in command of the regiment until after Lieutenant-Colonel Cavada's capture, and that consequently the report of all that precedes is compiled solely from my own observations and memory.

It affords me great pleasure to testify to the great gallantry and cool courage of Brigadier-General Graham, commanding the First Brigade, First Division, Third Corps, of which my regiment is a part, and to express my regret, in which I am joined by all the officers in my regiment, at his having been wounded, and trust that, his wound proving slight, he will soon return to again lead us to victory.

I am also happy to be able to mentions Captains [Francis] Fix and Eddy, the former of whom received a painful wound, and also Lieutenants Robinson, Newlin, and

A. W. Fix, for their bravery and efficient assistance during the engagement.

UNIT: 69th Infantry. **OTHER NAME:** "Second California."

ORGANIZATION: II Corps, 2nd Div., 2nd Brig.

RAISED: Philadelphia County.
MUSTERED: Camp Owen, Philadelphia, Aug., 19, 1861.

COMMANDER: 1) Col. Dennis O'Kane (1824-1863), mortally wounded in action on July 3rd. 2) Capt. William Davis (1832-1883).

MONUMENT LOCATION: At the Angle, 280 yards west of the Emmitsburg Road on Cemetery Ridge. (Note the company markers strung along the stonewall west of the Copse of Trees.) **MAP:** V, C-5..

STRENGTH: 10 Cos, 284 effectives. **LOSSES:** K-40, W-8, M-17. Total: 137. Percent Loss: 48.2.

WEAPONS: .58 Springfields, .577 Enfields, & .69 Smoothbores.

SUMMARY: Held the stone wall indicated by the position of their monument and company markers. Accepted the attack of Wright's Georgia and portions of Posey's Mississippi Brigade, as they advanced up the Cemetery Ridge from the Emmitsburg Road and captured an artillery battery posted 50 yards in advance of the 69th's position. Helped to stop the enemy advance, then counter-charged with the brigade, driving the enemy out of the battery and west toward the Emmitsburg Road. Captured many prisoners, losing 28 men in the process. Returned to their position with skirmishers west of the Emmitsburg Road.

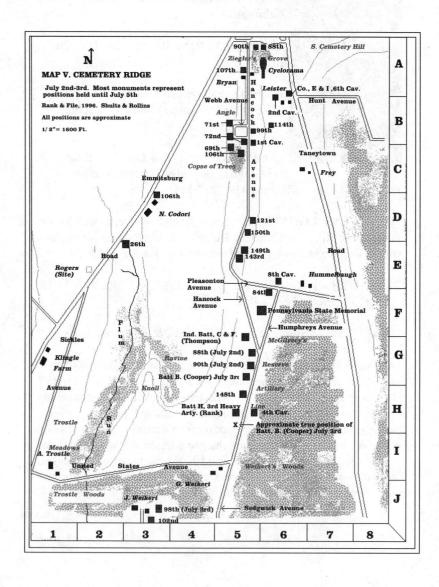

MAP V. CEMETERY RIDGE

July 2nd-3rd. Most monuments represent positions held until July 5th

Rank & File, 1996. Shultz & Rollins

All positions are approximate

1/2" = 1600 Ft.

Report of Capt. William Davis. Sixty-ninth Pennsylvania Infantry. Jones' Cross Roads, Md., July 12, 1863

Captain: In compliance with an order from Brigadier General Webb, we took up our line of position behind a temporary breastwork made of fence rails, strengthened with stone, on the morning of July 2, and remained in that position till the enemy advanced upon us, about 4 o'clock in the afternoon. The battery of the First Rhode Island being immediately in our front, had kept up a fierce cannonading for two hours before, and doubtless had done great execution on the rebel lines. This fact rendered our position a mark of no insignificance. The capture of the battery became a matter of great importance to the rebels, as future events proved fully. Onward they came, and absolutely seized upon the cannon. To prevent this, all the energy and power that could be brought to bear against such a result were brought into requisition. Our men fought with the bravery and coolness of veterans, and, after fighting with desperation for a period of one hour or more, we had the satisfaction of seeing the rebels turn and flee in a perfect panic.

UNIT: 71st Infantry. **OTHER NAME:** "1st California Regiment."

ORGANIZATION: II Corps, 2nd Div., 2nd Brig.

RAISED: Philadelphia & New York City. **MUSTERED:** Fort Schuyler, New York City. June 1861.

COMMANDER: Col. Richard P. Smith, Jr. (1837-1887).

MONUMENT LOCATION: At the Angle, 280 yards west of Hancock Ave. on Cemetery Ridge. This monument represents the position occupied by portions of the regiment, skirmishers not included, during the battle of Gettysburg, including their action near Culp's Hill. **MAP:** V, B-5.

STRENGTH: 10 cos, 261 effectives. **LOSSES:** K-21, W-58, M-19. Total: 98. Percent Loss: 37.5.

WEAPONS: .58 Springfields.

SUMMARY: Posted on top of Cemetery Ridge in rear of the Copse of Trees. Advanced to the stone wall to the right of the 69th Infantry, in front of Cushing's 4th U.S. Artillery. Occupied the position indicated by their present monument, (moving southwest) counter-attacking toward the Codori farm. Moved forward following the 106th Pennsylvania to the Emmitsburg Road, recapturing one cannon from Brown's Rhode Island Battery in the process. Returned to the crest of Cemetery Ridge where the regiment was detached from the brigade and ordered to follow Carroll's Brigade to reinforce the XI Corps on East Cemetery Hill. Misdirected, the regiment became lost in the darkness and ended up near the Abram Spangler farm east of the Baltimore Pike, a full 500 yards south of Cemetery Hill. As ordered, they continued east past the Spangler farm into some woods near today's Geary Ave. and the Pardee Field. Nearly flanked and surrounded by advanced portions of the Stonewall Brigade, they pulled back to the Baltimore Pike. Against orders, left their position and reported back to Webb's brigade, leaving open direct access to the Baltimore Pike for the enemy, which was not exploited in the dark. (Some thought that Smith should have been court-martialed for his actions at the Spangler Farm.) Retook their original position on top of the ridge in rear of the Copse of Trees.

Report of Col. R. Penn Smith, Seventy-first Pennsylvania Infantry Jones Cross-Roads, MD., July 12, 1863.
CAPTAIN: In the afternoon of the 2d instant, I went to the support of the Sixty-ninth Pennsylvania Volunteers, then on the front, and became engaged with the enemy, taking some 20 prisoners and retaking a brass cannon and limber which the enemy held.
About dark of this day, by an order through Captain Duffy, I was ordered to the support of a portion of the Eleventh Corps. Having arrived on the ground, I could find no general to report to who had command of any one portion of the troops. An adjutant-general directed me to proceed to the front, assuring me that all was safe on either flank. Arriving at the front, I became engaged with the enemy on the front. At the same time he attacked me on my right and rear. I immediately ordered my command to retire to the road in my

rear, when I returned to camp against orders. During the engagement, I lost 3 commissioned officers and 11 enlisted men.

UNIT: 72nd Infantry. **OTHER NAME:** "Third California," "Baxter's Fire Zouaves."

ORGANIZATION: II Corps, 2nd Div., 2nd Brig.

RAISED: Philadelphia. **MUSTERED:** Camp Lyon, Philadelphia, Aug. 10, 1861.

COMMANDER: 1) Col. Dewitt C. Baxter (1829-1881), wounded on July 2nd. 1) Lt. Col. Theodore Hesser (1829-1863), assumed command on Baxter's wounding, KIA in action at Mine Run.

MONUMENT LOCATION: 1) On Cemetery Ridge 280 feet west of Hancock Ave., a few feet south of the Angle. This monument represents the advanced position occupied by a few of its men for a few moments on the repulse of Pickett's Charge. (See Pennsylvania State Supreme Court case concerning the placement of this monument, parts of which are in Richard Rollins, ed., *Pickett's Charge: Eyewitness Accounts*). 2) Located at the Copse of Trees on the west shoulder of Hancock Ave. This monument represents more accurately the line the regiment held on both days of action at Gettysburg. **MAP: V, B-5.**

STRENGTH: 10 Cos, 380 effectives. **LOSSES:** K-44, W-146, M-2. Total: 192. Percent Loss: 50.5.

WEAPONS: .58 Springfields & Austrians, & .577 Enfields.

SUMMARY: Advanced from its position in rear of the Copse of Trees, near their No. 2 monument, following the 71st Pa. toward the stone wall in front of the Copse of Trees. Secured their place at the stone wall at their No. 1 monument, as the 69th and 71st crossed over the wall moving west. Held their position without becoming fully engaged. Withdrew as the 69th and 71st returned, going into position again in rear of the Copse of Trees near their No. 2 monument on Hancock Ave.

Report of Lieut. Col. Theodore Hesser, Seventy-second Penn-sylvania Infantry. Jones' Cross-Roads, MD., July 11, 1863. CAPTAIN: On the 2d instant, the regiment supported a battery until 6 p.m., when (the first line of battle giving way) orders were received to advance and assist in reoccupying the ground lost, which orders were executed without, how-ever, becoming directly engaged.

UNIT: 106th Infantry. **OTHER NAME:** "Fifth California."

ORGANIZATION: II Corps, 2nd Div., 2nd Brig.

RAISED: From the counties of Bradford, Lycoming, Montgomery, & Philadelphia. **MUSTERED:** Bull's Head, Philadelphia, Sept., 1861.

COMMANDER: Lt. Col. William L. Curry (1833-1864), KIA at Spotsylvania.

MONUMENT LOCATIONS: 1) On Cemetery Ridge in rear of the Copse of Trees along Hancock Ave., representing two days' action. 2) On East Cemetery Hill, representing the regiment's forward position after its engagement at the No. 1 monument on Cemetery Ridge. **MAP:** V, C-5 & VII, A-4.

STRENGTH: 10 Cos, 280 effectives. **LOSSES:** K-9, W-54, M-1. Total: 64. Percent Loss: 22.9.

WEAPONS: .58 Springfields & French .69 Smoothbores.

SUMMARY: Waited in reserve posted to the left rear of the Copse of Trees on Cemetery Ridge, near today's No. 1 monument, and engaged with skirmishers along the Em-mitsburg Road. When Wright's Georgia Brigade drove their skirmishers back toward the Copse of Trees, the rest of the regiment moved forward to the stonewall. As ordered, moved north skirting the wall, then by left flank, advanced over the wall with fixed bayonets, and charged oblique to the southwest toward the Codori farm, capturing many prisoners and driving the enemy back. Withdrew leaving companies A and B along the Emmitsburg Road as skirmishers. Reformed at No. 1 monument on Hancock Ave. Detached from Webb's brigade, less two companies, and advanced with Carroll's brigade to the east toward the Evergreen Cemetery, via today's Cyclorama and Visitor Center. Charged oblique from the southwest across the Baltimore Pike and into Rickett's and Wiedrich's over-run batteries. Continued through the batteries pressing portions of Hays' Louisiana Brigade off the crest back through the utility company yard. Reformed at the stonewall along the base of North Cemetery Hill, brought back with them several dozen prisoners. Pulled back to the northern crest of East Cemetery Hill near their present monument south of the utility company. Remained here for the balance of the battle less two companies on Cemetery Ridge.

Report of Lieut. Col. William L. Curry, One hundred and sixth Pennsylvania Infantry. Jones' Cross-Roads, MD., July 11, 1863.

CAPTAIN: After arriving upon the ground the morning of the 2d instant, by order of General Webb the regiment was placed in position near the front and center of the line. Two companies (A and B) were deployed as skirmishers in front of the line. They were warmly engaged until the action became general. The coolness and intrepidity with which they were handled kept the enemy at bay, and reflects great credit upon the officers and men of these two companies. Our left having attacked the enemy, were, after a desperate conflict, compelled to retire.

At this time the enemy opened upon our lines a furious cannonade, wounding one of our officers and several men. Under cover of this fire they advanced their infantry, driving back our first line, and forcing the artillery on my immediate front to withdraw. By order of Brigadier-General Webb, I advanced the regiment by the left flank, and formed in rear of the second line. Shortly after, orders were received to move forward. I advanced the regiment to the crest of the hill, and opened fire upon the enemy. After several volleys, perceiving that we checked his advance, and seeing his lines waver, I ordered bayonets fixed and a charge to be made, which movement resulted in a complete success, the enemy retiring in confusion to his original position in the woods. We pursued the fleeing enemy to the Emmitsburg road, when, perceiving that we were separated from the line on our left by a space of 70 yards, and having no troops on our right, excepting the remnant of the Eighty-second New York Volunteers, I halted the regiment, and sent to the rear for support, having first deployed skirmishers on my front. The officer whom I sent not returning, I left the regiment in charge of Major Stover, and personally applied to General Webb for support, and I was ordered to withdraw the regiment to its original position.

In the charge we made, we recovered three guns which had been abandoned. I sent them to the rear by hand. We also captured and sent to the rear about 250 prisoners, among whom were 1 colonel ([William] Gibson, Forty-eighth Georgia), 5 captains, and 15 lieutenants.

Ten minutes after we returned, the firing not having ceased upon the right, we were ordered to proceed in the direction of the firing, and report to Major-General Howard, commanding the Eleventh Corps, who assigned us to the command of General Ames, by whose order we were placed in the front line, on the right of the Gettysburg road and near the cemetery. We remained there until the morning of July 4, having been exposed to a very severe and concentrated fire from three batteries.

On the morning of the 3d, I detailed a body of sharpshooters, who, under cover of the houses in the vicinity, kept up a continuous fire upon the enemy's sharpshooters, who were picking off the gunners of our batteries. I have reason to believe that the enemy's sharpshooters suffered considerably from this body of men. . . .

I will add that the two skirmishing companies detailed on the morning of the 2d did not accompany the regiment to the right, but remained in the center, and took an active part in the engagement on the afternoon of the 3d.

Early in the engagement, Adj. F. M. Pleis was severely wounded and Lieut. John A. Steel was ordered to act as adjutant. Adjt. F. M. Pleis, while on the field, by his daring courage and example to the men, contributed much to the success which attended us. His successor, Lieut. John A. Steel, by his example and disregard of danger, rendered valuable services on the field, and is entitled to more than a passing notice.

I make especial mention of Maj. John H. Stover, who, by his coolness and daring, rendered much valuable assistance. I also bear willing testimony to the good conduct of Capts. John J. Sperry, R. H. Ford, and James C. Lynch, and Lieut. C. S. Schwartz. In fact, the same may be said of every officer in my command.

2ND CITATION, JULY 2ND: 121st Infantry.

GENERAL INFORMATION & DATA: See 121st Infantry, July 1st.

MONUMENT LOCATION: On the east shoulder of Hancock Ave. approximately 150 yards due south of the Copse of trees. Map V, D-5.

SUMMARY: Moved with the brigade over the stone wall in rear of the Vermont B.rigade, advancing toward Codori's farm. Helped secure the left section of Brown's Rhode Island Battery. Pulled back to the position indicated by the monument for the rest of the night.

2nd CITATION, JULY 2ND & 3rd: 142nd Infantry.

GENERAL INFORMATION & DATA: See 142nd Infantry on July 1.

MONUMENT LOCATION: None.

SUMMARY FOR JULY 2ND: Advanced with the brigade keeping in rear of the main Federal line. Went into position in reserve on Cemetery Ridge, near the present monument dedicated to the 121st Pennsylvania, 150 yards south of the Copse of Trees on the east shoulder of Hancock Ave, Skirmishers advanced across the Emmitsburg Road due west of the Codori Farm, met with heavy enemy fire and returned to Plum Run to establish a reserve picket line. Held their position for the remainder of the night. On July 3rd the regiment held the above position by the 121st monument, only to be detached at 2:00 p.m. and moved south to the George Weikert woods. Held in reserve during Pickett's Charge. Light engagement.

Report We remained in the same position until the evening of the 2d, when with the regiment of Colonel Biddle (One hundred and twenty-first Pennsylvania Volunteers), we were required to remove to the opposite side of the road. The men lay on their arms during the night but a few rods from their previous resting-place. Early in the forenoon of the 3d, my command was formed in line with the One hundred and twenty-first Pennsylvania Volunteers on the western side of the road, about 50 rods to the left of the former position. About 2 p.m. the enemy opened a very severe artillery fire on our front and along the whole line. This was followed by a general advance of their infantry. When the latter movement took place, my regiment, with the approval of General Rowley, was advanced to a rude breastwork of rails on the right of the Second Brigade. Another line of our forces lay in front of us. The advance of the enemy at this point was met so promptly and gallantly by the troops in the first line, that the men of my command had neither occasion nor opportunity to do more than fire an occasional shot at a few sharpshooters, who, from covered positions, were trying to pick off the artillerymen in a battery immediately in our rear. The attacking column was completely destroyed or captured, without having materially disturbed the line of our forces in front of this position, and without having made it necessary for the second line, in which we were placed, to participate in the fight. We remained in the same position until 9 p.m., when we were relieved by other troops, and the regiment was withdrawn to a point near the road to rest during the night.

Although my small command was exposed, in common with the rest of the brigade, to a severe artillery fire during the afternoon of the 3d, in addition to an occasional fire of less intensity during the whole of the previous day, we have no serious casualties to report. Two men only were slightly wounded by the explosion of a shell on the afternoon of the 3d. The fall of Capt. C. H. Flagg, of this regiment, who was a member of General Rowley's staff, and who was killed by a shell on the evening of the 3d, does not come properly within the scope of this report; but I cannot refrain from saying that his loss is deeply deplored by the company which he had long ably led, and by all others who knew him. While it is true that my remnant of a regiment had but little part in the great results of July 2 and 3, I am glad to say that the officers and men exhibited commendable firmness, and were ready cheerfully to undergo greater trials than fell to their lot.

2ND CITATION, JULY 2ND: 88th Infantry.

GENERAL INFORMATION & DATA: See 88th Infantry, July 1st.

MONUMENT LOCATION: 1) Located on the west shoulder of Hancock Ave., about 20 yards south of its intersection with Humphreys Ave. on the crest of South Cemetery Ridge, normally referred to as McGilvery's line. Map: V, G-5.

SUMMARY: Followed the 90th Infantry from Cemetery Hill to reinforce the III Corps. Skirmishers were sent forward as Willard's brigade withdrew from the Plum Run, occupying a small knoll between Plum Run to the west and a small ravine to the east, a few yards in advance of the main Federal line. Lightly engaged as the skirmishers, along with Berdan's Sharpshooters, traded shots with skirmishers from Barksdale's Mississippi Brigade posted in the Trostle meadows. No casualties recorded. Moved north to Ziegler's Grove near midnight.

Report of Capt. Edmund Y. Patterson, Eighty-eighth Pennsylvania Infantry. August 22, 1863.
July 2.—Were moved about to different parts of the battlefield, but were not engaged in musketry. July 3 —At daybreak, were behind a stone wall on Cemetery Hill, behind part of the Eleventh Corps. Batteries soon became engaged, and a few of our men were wounded. About 2 p.m. the enemy opened upon us from all sides. We were then at the foot of Cemetery Hill, and were compelled to change our position for safety during the heaviest of the fire. About 6 p.m. we were run double-quick to the center, where we found hard

fighting had been progressing. We immediately threw up breastworks of rails, and part of the regiment was ordered out on picket, where the enemy's sharpshooters annoyed us and wounded several.

2ND CITATION, JULY 2ND: 90th Infantry.

GENERAL INFORMATION AND DATA: See July 1st.

MONUMENT LOCATION: On the west shoulder of Hancock Ave., about 40 yards south of its intersection with Humphery's Ave., on South Cemetery Ridge. **MAP:** V, G-7.

SUMMARY: As ordered, marched from Cemetery Hill to the position indicated near monument, to reinforce the III Corps. Held this position sending skirmishers forward when Willard's II Corps brigade withdrew from the Plum Run, and occupied a small knoll between Plum Run to the west, and a small ravine to the east, several yards in front of the main Federal line. Lightly engaged with only a few men slightly wounded. Moved toward Ziegler's Grove sometime near midnight.

2ND CITATION, JULY 2ND: 107th Infantry.

GENERAL INFORMATION & DATA: See 107th Infantry, July 1st.

LOCATION OF MONUMENT: Located on Hancock Avenue north of the Bryan barn in Zeigler's Grove. Map: V, A-5.

SUMMARY: Moved to various positions on Cemetery Hill in support of artillery and the 11th Corps. Advanced to the left, (southwest) toward the Copse of Trees on the repulse of Wright's Georgia and portions of Posey's Mississippi Brigades. Several men wounded by artillery on their advance. Collected prisoners and cared for wounded. Returned to Ziegler's Grove after dark to the position indicated by their monument on Cemetery Ridge, located west of Hancock Avenue, just a few feet north of the Bryan barn, and about 40 yards west of the Cyclorama. Held this position throughout the night of July 2nd.

The following is the report of Lieut. Col. J. MacThomson, of the One hundred and seventh Pennsylvania Volunteers, during the action of July 1, at Gettysburg, he being in command up to that time. July 2. — During the forenoon we were relieved by the Third Division, Second Corps, and taken a few hundred yards in the rear to support a battery. We lay on our arms until about 6.30 p.m., when we were marched to the left, toward the Round Top, under a heavy and effective fire, to assist in driving the rebel hordes back in the famous charge of the second day of the fight. After the charge, we marched back to near the cemetery, and were ordered to lay in rear of a stout fence, being a protection for the men from the enemy's sharpshooters in our front. Our casualties during the second day were 1 commissioned officer and several men wounded. Our strength was about 78 guns and 12 commissioned officers.

UNIT: 1st Cavalry. **OTHER NAME:** "15th Reserves," "44th Volunteers."

ORGANIZATION: Cavalry Corps, 2nd Div., 1st Brig. 10 companies detached to Army Headquarters, one company detached to VI Corps Headquarters.

RAISED: From the Counties of Allegheny, Berks, Centre, Clinton, Fayette, Greene, Juniata, Mifflin, & Montgomery. **MUSTERED:** Camp Jones, Washington D.C., Aug., 28, 1861.

COMMANDER: Col. John P. Taylor (1827-1914).

MONUMENT LOCATION: On the east shoulder of Hancock Ave., 20 yards east of the Copse of Trees on Cemetery Ridge. MAP: V, C-5.

STRENGTH: 11 Cos, 355 effectives. **LOSSES:** K-0, W-0, M-2. Total: 2. Percent Loss: 0.6.

WEAPONS: Sharps & Burnside Carbines, Colt .44s.

SUMMARY: Detached from McIntosh's cavalry brigade, less Company H, left at VI Corps Headquarters. Some of the regiment arrived on the battlefield after midnight on July 2nd escorting Meade into the Evergreen Cemetery. By midmorning on the 2nd the regiment was in position along the Taneytown Road in reserve. Used principally to guard headquarters and the surrounding area about the Leister House on the Taneytown Road. Several companies detached as orderlies and couriers.
No report filed.

UNIT: 2nd Cavalry. **OTHER NAME:** "59th Volunteers".

ORGANIZATION: Army Headquarters Guard.

RAISED: From the Counties of Armstrong, Centre, Crawford, Lancaster, Northampton, Philadelphia & Tioga.
MUSTERED: Camp Patterson, Philadelphia, Dec., 1861.

COMMANDER: Col. Richard B. Price (1807-1876).

MONUMENT LOCATION: Located 60 yards west of the Taneytown Road at Army Headquarters (Leister House) on Cemetery Ridge, 60 yards due south of today's Cyclorama building. MAP: **V, B-6.**

STRENGTH: 10 Cos, 575 effectives. **LOSSES:** None.

WEAPONS: Sharps Carbines & Colt .44s.

SUMMARY: Attached to Army Headquarters, the regiment was split up in various areas as the army moved into Gettysburg. The first elements of the regiment arrived at Meade's headquarters shortly after the Leister house was chosen for the Army Headquarters on the morning of July 2nd. Spent all of July 2nd moving about the battlefield as orderlies and aides. The Leister barnyard was used as the regimental headquarters.

UNIT: 4th Cavalry. **OTHER NAME:** "64th Volunteers."

ORGANIZATION: Cavalry Corps, 2nd Div., 3rd Brig., detached to Army Headquarters.

RAISED: From the Counties of Allegheny, Lebanon, Luzerne. Venango & Westmoreland. **MUSTERED:** Camp Curtin, Harrisburg. Oct. 30, 1861.

COMMANDER: Lt. Col. William E. Doster (1837-1919).

MONUMENT LOCATION: On Cemetery Ridge on the east shoulder of Hancock Avenue approximately 400 yards south of the Pennsylvania monument at a position on McGilvery's Artillery line. **MAP:** V, H-5.

STRENGTH: 12 Cos, 304 effectives. **LOSSES:** K-1, W-0, M-0. Total: .1. Percent loss: .4.

WEAPONS: Sharps Carbines, Colt .36 & .44s.

SUMMARY: Arrived at Gettysburg in the early morning hours of July 2nd, going into position along the Baltimore Pike south of Rock Creek. Detached to Army Headquarters in the forenoon, posted in the George Weikert woods, approximately three quarters of a mile south of Meade's Headquarters, (Leister House) on Cemetery Ridge. Held in reserve throughout the afternoon of Longstreet's first assault. The 4th moved forward, dismounted, in support of batteries commanded by Lt. Col. Freeman McGilvery, assembled on the ridge at approximately 8:00 p.m. Did not engage. Several companies detached to escort prisoners from the front. Moved back into the woods near the Taneytown Road for the remainder of the night. Held this position through July 5th in support of McGilvery's artillery line. Did not engage. Details were sent to bury dead and collect arms.

UNIT: 6th Cavalry. **OTHER NAME:** "Rush's Lancers," "70th Volunteers."

ORGANIZATION: Cavalry Corps, 1st Div., Reserve Brigade. Companies E & I detached to Army Headquarters. Companies A, D, & F detached elsewhere during Gettysburg Campaign.

RAISED: From the Counties of Berks & Philadelphia. **MUSTERED:** Camp Meigs, Philadelphia, Oct. 31,1861.

COMMANDER: Maj. James H. Haseltine (1833-1907).

MONUMENT LOCATION: 1) On the Taneytown Road at Army Headquarters, (Leister house) Cemetery Ridge. This monument represents companies E & I who were detached to Army Headquarters as orderlies and aides. 2) Near the South Cavalry Battlefield on the east shoulder of the Emmitsburg Road, approximately three miles south of Gettysburg. Represents temporary position of July 1. Not engaged. **MAP:** V, A-6 &. VII, G-7.

STRENGTH: 9 Cos, 242 effectives. **LOSSES:** K-3, W-7, M-2. Total: 12. Percent Loss: 5.0.

WEAPONS: Sharps Carbines, Colt .36 & .44s.

SUMMARY: Detached from Merritt's brigade, less companies E & I at Army Headquarters, the regiment escorted 2nd Corps trains toward Gettysburg. Joined Gregg's division of cavalry at Frederick, Maryland, moved quickly to Gettysburg. Arrived late on the afternoon of July 1st. Immediately sent back to Manchester to continue protecting trains. Companies E & I arrived at Meade's headquarters on the morning of July 2nd as ordered. Served as guards and orderlies indicated by the monument at the Leister house.

JULY 2ND: 1st Light, Battery B.

GENERAL INFORMATION & DATA: See 1st Light, Battery B, July 1st.

MONUMENT LOCATION: Atop the crest of East Cemetery Hill due east of the Baltimore Pike across from the Evergreen Cemetery gatehouse. Represents the position occupied throughout the day of July 2nd and up until the near repulse of Hays' and Avery's brigades on their charge up Cemetery Hill. **Map:** VII, B-4.

SUMMARY: Held this position with three serviceable cannons, one being disabled on July 1st. Engaged in light counter-battery fire throughout the forenoon becoming extreme during the mid-afternoon. Their position was hammered from the north and northeast during the cannonade prior to Hays' and Avery's attack. Heavy casualties were taken as the Confederates launched their infantry attack. Ordered out, Cooper could not disengage due to the severe pounding he was getting. A 20-pound Parrott battery to his rear caused extensive damage as one round exploded prematurely over Cooper's line during their withdrawal. His exodus was slow but orderly, pulling out of line just moments before the infantry attack began and moved back to the Artillery Park south of Powers Hill.

Report At about sunset in the evening. having refilled the ammunition chests, the battery was placed in position, by order of Colonel Wainwright, on the crest of the hill in rear of Gettysburg, and fronting to the northeast. The battery remained in this position without firing until 9.30 a.m., July 2, when occasional shots were fired at small bodies of the enemy's infantry and cavalry which were maneuvering in the skirts of timber from 1 mile to 1 1/2 miles distant until 4 p.m., when the enemy brought a number of 10 and 20 pounder Parrott guns into position in the open field about 1,400 and 2,000 yards distant, and opened a vigorous fire upon the position. To this fire the battery replied, and, with the assistance of a battery on its left, Reynolds' and Stevens' batteries on the right, the enemy's guns were silenced in about two and a half hours' firing. The battery fired occasional shots into the position of these batteries until about 7 p.m., when it was relieved by Captain Ricketts' battery, and ordered by Colonel Wainwright to report to General Tyler, commanding Artillery Reserve, to refit and fill ammunition chests, one gun having been dismounted late in this day's engagement. I was again ready for action by 11 a. m., but, receiving no orders, the battery remained in General Tyler's camp until the 3d instant.

The casualties of this day's engagement were: Private J. H. McCleary, killed; Private P. G. Hoagland, killed; Private Jesse Temple, wounded severely; Private J. C. Cornelius, wounded slightly; Private D. W. Taylor, wounded slightly; Corpl. Joseph Reed, wounded slightly: 1 horse killed, 2 horses disabled. About 500 rounds of ammunition were expended. On the afternoon of the 3d instant, about .3 p.m., during a heavy cannonade, the battery was ordered into position among the batteries in the Second Corps front and immediately opened upon a shattered battery of the enemy which was firing on our front. This battery soon ceased or withdrew. The battery ceased firing for one-half hour, when a line of the enemy's infantry appeared, approaching over the crest of a hill about 1,000 yards distant. Into this line this battery, in connection with the adjacent batteries, fired case shot until they reached canister range, when a few charges were fired into them, completely routing them, without any infantry assistance. The casualties of this day's engagement were: Private Frederick Workman, wounded slightly. About 150 rounds of ammunition were expended in this day's engagement. The battery remained in this position until the afternoon of July 5, when, by order of Colonel Wainwright, it rejoined the Artillery Brigade. The total of ammunition expended in these three days' engagements was 1,000 rounds.

UNIT: 1st Artillery, Batteries F & G Consolidated. **OTHER NAME:** "Ricketts'."

ORGANIZATION: 3rd Volunteer Artillery Reserve Brigade.

JULY 2

RAISED: Battery F, Schuylkill, Battery G, Philadelphia.
MUSTERED: Camp Curtin, Harrisburg, Aug. 5, 1861.

COMMANDER: Capt. Robert B. Ricketts (1839-1918).

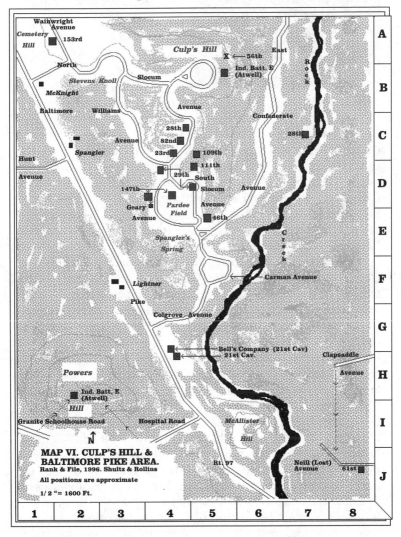

MONUMENT LOCATION: Atop the crest of East Cemetery Hill directly east of the Baltimore Pike and National Cemetery. This monument and cannons represent the battery's position during their action on July 2nd as well as July 3rd.
MAP: VII, B-4.

STRENGTH: 2 Cos, 144 effectives. **LOSSES:** K-6, W-14, M-3, Total: 23. Percent Loss: 16.0.

WEAPONS: Six 3 inch-Ordnance Rifles.

SUMMARY: The first unit to respond to Maj. Thomas Osborn's request (third actual request) for more batteries for Cemetery Hill. Ricketts' led the Third Reserve Brigade out of the Artillery Park and north up the Taneytown Road toward Cemetery Hill, arriving near today's Visitor Center. Ordered to East Cemetery Hill, Ricketts led his battery through the swale housing today's "Battlefield Tower," just south of Cemetery Hill toward the Baltimore Pike. All the other batteries attached to his brigade moved onto Cemetery Hill via the Taneytown Road across from the Visitor Center. Ricketts' moved onto the Baltimore Pike facing due north in column of sections, waiting in rear of some woods south of Cemetery Hill. Ricketts sat for approximately two hours waiting to relieve Cooper who could not pull out. Heavy enemy cannonading from the north and northeast exploded in the woods just east of Ricketts, whose position was near today's intersection of North Slocum Avenue and the Baltimore Pike. Finally pulling into Cooper's vacated position, Ricketts unlimbered under light artillery fire, as most of the enemy guns were now silenced. Confederate infantry showed itself within minutes of Ricketts' entrance advancing from two angles toward the battery. Ricketts ignored the counter-battery fire and focused his attention on the closing gray lines. The Confederate attack hit Ricketts from three directions: 1) from due north through today's water tower and Wiedrich's battery markers. 2) from the northeast, and 3) from southeast. Overrun from his left flank, the gunners fought in vicious hand-to-hand combat for fifteen minutes trying to recapture the battery. Reinforced, the artillerymen helped in the recapture of the entire battery, as well as Wiedrich's New York battery to Ricketts' left. Resecued, with one gun spiked and disabled, Ricketts continued to hold his position through the night.

JULY 2

Report of Capt. R. Bruce Ricketts, Batteries F and G, First Pennsylvania Light Artillery. Hdqrs. Batteries F and G, First Pa. Artillery, August 30, 1863.

CAPTAIN: At 4 p.m. I was ordered by Captain Huntington to report to Col. C. S. Wainwright, First New York Artillery, who placed me in position on Cemetery Hill, to the right of the turnpike leading into Gettysburg. During the afternoon, I was engaged with the batteries on the enemy's left, and in shelling a column of the enemy that charged into the woods on my right, which was occupied by the Twelfth Army Corps. At about 8 p.m. a heavy column of the enemy charged on my battery, and succeeded in capturing and spiking my left piece. The cannoneers fought them hand to hand with handspikes, rammers, and pistols, and succeeded in checking them for a moment, when a part of the Second Army Corps charged in and drove them back. During the charge I expended every round of canister in the battery, and then fired case shot without the fuses. The enemy suffered severely.

During the battle of July 3, I was engaged with the batteries on the enemy's left and center. During the battle of the 2d and 3d, I expended 1,200 rounds of ammunition

First Lieut. C. B. Brockway, Battery F, First Pennsylvania Artillery, First Lieut. Beldin Spence, Battery G, First Pennsylvania Artillery, and First Sergt. Francis H. Snider, fought their sections with the greatest gallantry.

UNIT: Independent Battery E. **OTHER NAME:** "Knaps."

ORGANIZATION: XII Corps Artillery Brigade.

RAISED: Allegheny & Philadelphia counties. **MUSTERED:** Camp De Korponay, Point of Rocks, Maryland. Sept. 1, 1861.

COMMANDER: Lt. Charles A. Atwell (1840-1863), mortally wounded at Wauhatchie, Tennessee.

MONUMENT LOCATION: 1) In the woods atop Powers Hill (pictured). 2) Atop Culp's Hill. Both represent positions

occupied by portions of the battery on July 1st, 2nd or 3rd.
MAP: VI, H-2 & B-5.

STRENGTH: 139 effectives. **LOSSES:** K-0, W-3, M-0.
Total: 3. Percent Loss: 2.2.

WEAPONS: Six 10-pounder Parrott Rifles.

SUMMARY: Arrived on the field in the late afternoon of July
1st near Rock Creek. Moved immediately to the position
indicated by their 1st monument on the north brow of
Powers Hill. (The hill at the time of battle was virtually free
of timber, allowing the gunners a full field of fire to the north,
northeast and east.) Held this position throughout July
2nd. One gun was rushed to Culp's Hill at dusk and pulled
by hand up the small logging road to the summit to the
position indicated by the No. 2 monument, followed thirty
minutes later by another section. The half battery opened
with good effect on Confederate batteries posted 1500 yards
away on south Benner's Hill, driving at least one enemy
battery from their position. Held this position until late at
night when ordered to return to Powers Hill.

2ND CITATION, JULY 2ND: 153rd infantry.

GENERAL INFORMATION & DATA: See
153rd Infantry, July 1st.

**LOCATION OF MONUMENT (S) OR MARK-
ERS:** Located at the base of East Cemetery
Hill on the west shoulder of Wainwright
Ave., approximately 150 yards north of Slocum Ave. Rep-
resents the position occupied by the regiment on the repulse
of Avery's brigade. **Map:** VI, A-2 & VII, C-5.

SUMMARY FOR JULY 2ND: Their original position was
atop East Cemetery Hill, about 100 yards east of their
present-day monument near the monument dedicated to
Reynold's New York Battery L. Manned a heavy skirmish
line at the base of the hill along the stone wall bordering the
east shoulder of Wainwright Avenue, across from their
present monument. Avery's attack raced around their
flanks and up the slope. The left flank was pushed back as

Federal regiments on that part of the line gave way, allowing many Confederates to exploit the break. The right flank was secured by devastating fire support from a hidden Maine battery and a Massachusetts regiment posted to the right front of the 153rd. Very few North Carolinians made it to the crest of East Cemetery Hill through the 153rd's skirmish and main lines. Most enemy obliqued to the northwest while moving up the slope, just south of Ricketts' monument, angling for the battery. The 153rd's line counter-charged with II Corps reinforcements, driving the few enemy off the slope and back east of the stone wall. The surviving skirmishers faced north and cut off many retreating enemy soldiers. Friendly fire wounded several men from the 153rd skirmish line. The entire regiment was reformed in the lane near their present monument, and held this position for the balance of the battle. Skirmishers sent toward the Culp farm were kept busy throughout the remainder of July 2nd and 3rd. The regiment held this position until July 5th as most of the 11th Corps regiments moved toward the town. Details were sent to the Culp farm on July 4th to aid enemy wounded and collect captured arms.

2ND CITATION, JULY 2ND: 27th Infantry.

GENERAL INFORMATION & DATA: See 27th infantry, July 1st.

MONUMENT LOCATION: On the north crest of East Cemetery Hill due south of the water company east of the Baltimore Pike, represents the position occupied during the repulse of Hays' Louisiana Brigade. Their original position is not exact due to extensive damage by the utility company's excavation, which significantly altered the ground over which they terminated their charge. **Map:** VII, A-3.

SUMMARY FOR JULY 2ND: Occupied a position inside the Evergreen Cemetery in support of batteries posted on Cemetery Hill. Ordered forward by General Howard, along with the 73rd Pa. to assist in a counter-charge to dislodge the enemy on East Cemetery Hill. Charged on the left of the 73rd, oblique from the southwest past Cooper's Pennsylvania battery's just-vacated position, and into Wiedrich's overrun New York battery, posted 20 yards east of the Baltimore Pike. Fought hand-to-hand with a Louisiana Brigade amongst Wiedrich's guns, driving the enemy out of the battery and back through today's water company and down to the base of Cemetery Hill. Spent the remainder of the night under arms at the position indicated by their monument.

2ND CITATION, JULY 2ND: 73rd Infantry.

GENERAL INFORMATION & DATA: See 73rd Infantry, July 1st.

MONUMENT LOCATION: A few yards east of the Baltimore Pike across from the Evergreen Cemetery Gatehouse on East Cemetery Hill, represents the position occupied during Hays' and Avery's assault on Cemetery Hill, as well as July 3rd to 5th. **Map:** VII, B-3.

SUMMARY: Originally posted somewhere in the Evergreen Cemetery in support of batteries on the hill, ordered by General Howard, along with the 27th Pa., to assist in a counter-charge to repulse the enemy who were now atop East Cemetery Hill. Charged oblique from the southwest, on the right of the 27th, crossed the Baltimore Pike, and moved through Cooper's Pennsylvania battery's vacated position, where as a firing line was formed with men from Ricketts' overrun battery and other 11th Corps troops. Again advanced as II Corps reinforcements rushed past their line on the right. Helped recapture Ricketts' Pennsylvania battery by driving the enemy back off the crest into the dark. Reformed in the Baltimore Pike holding their place throughout the remainder of the battle near their present monument on East Cemetery Hill. Not engaged on July 3rd as a unit. Many men detailed to help work the undermanned batteries on Cemetery Hill. Exposed to the artillery crossfire during the great cannonade. Three men reportedly killed during the bombardment, one while helping serve a battery. Held this position until July 5th. Details formed to help bury the dead and collect arms, as well as search for their own missing and wounded from the battle of July 1st.

2ND CITATION, JULY 2ND: 56th Infantry.

GENERAL INFORMATION & DATA: See 56th Infantry July 1st.

MONUMENT LOCATION: Monument currently missing. The regiment's position was south of monument to Atwell's Independent Pennsylvania Battery E, located on the east shoulder of the North Slocum Ave. loop, atop Culp's Hill. **Map:** VI, A-5.

SUMMARY: Anchoring the right flank of Cutler's brigade, wheeled right and advanced to the southeast 50 yards, toward the entrenchments to the left of the present monument to the 78th New York regiment, which anchored the left flank of Green's XII Corps Brigade. Engaged the enemy who attacked up the hill from the direction of East Confederate Ave., holding their position while taking several killed and wounded. Replaced early in the morning of the 3rd by the 150th New York, returning to their original position to the right of Wadsworth's brigade near today's monument to Atwell's Ind. Pennsylvania Artillery, Battery E.

Report of Col. J. William Hoffmann, Fifty-sixth Pennsy-lvania Infantry. IN THE FIELD, July 11, 1863.

CAPTAIN: On the 2d instant, we engaged the enemy on the ridge in rear of the town. Our loss here was 2 enlisted men killed and 3 wounded. My officers and men did all that could be asked of brave men. Of the enlisted men it is but just to mention Corporal [Patrick] Burns, of Company D, acting color-bearer, who was wounded while gallantly waving the flag in the face of the enemy on the evening of the 2nd instant. Private [George] Nolter, of Company D, was successful in capturing a major of the rebel army on the morning of the 4th instant.

Of the officers wounded, Lieutenant Gordon, Company B, has since died.

UNIT: 109th Infantry. **OTHER NAME:** "Curtin Light Guards."

ORGANIZATION: XII Corps, 2nd Div., 2nd Brig.

RAISED: Philadelphia. **MUSTERED:** Nicetown, Philadelphia. May 1, 1862.

COMMANDER: Capt. Frederick L. Gimber (1836-1910).

MONUMENT LOCATION: On the east shoulder of North Slocum Ave., directly opposite the intersection of Geary and South Slocum Avenues, on Culp's Hill. Represents both July 2nd & 3rd. **MAP:** VI, C-5.

STRENGTH: 10 Cos, 149 effectives. **LOSSES:** K-3, W-6, M-1. Total: 10. Percent Loss: 6.7.

WEAPONS: .58 Springfields, & ,577 Enfields.

SUMMARY: Took position with the brigade near Powers Hill, somewhere near today's intersection of the Baltimore Pike and the Hospital Road. On the morning of July 2nd advanced with the brigade to Culp's Hill, building earthworks at the site of their monument on Slocum Ave., still clearly visible at the monument site. Held this position unengaged until ordered to the left center of the Federal line to support the III Crops. Returned to find the enemy in possession of their works. Withdrew about 100 yards to the west and took position behind a stone wall on the northwest edge of today's Pardee Field, just north of intersection of Geary Ave. and North and South Slocum Ave. Held this position throughout the night.

Report of Capt. Frederick L. Gimber, One hundred and ninth Pennsylvania Infantry. NEAR GETTYSBURG, PA., July 4, 1863.

SIR: On the morning of the 2d, the regiment assisted in

erecting breastworks in the woods 1 mile from Gettysburg, Pa., and took position behind them, remaining there until evening, then changing our position with the brigade to a field along the Gettysburg pike half a mile distant, being subjected to an artillery fire from the enemy. Arriving here, we were immediately ordered back to our breastworks, and, upon entering the woods, were suddenly fired upon, causing some surprise and temporary confusion. The fire was supposed to come from our own troops, the darkness causing the mistake. The regiment was quickly reformed, withdrawn, and taken by another route near the position we previously occupied, viz, the breastworks. Finding that during our brief absence the enemy had moved to the right, occupying the breastworks, we moved our position to the open ground between the stone fence and breastworks, our right resting near the former. We remained in this position all night, exchanging occasional shots with the enemy, our front being protected by a line of skirmishers.

UNIT: 29th Infantry. **OTHER NAME:** "Jackson Regiment."

ORGANIZATION: XII Corps. 2nd Div., 2nd Brig.

RAISED: Philadelphia County. **MUSTERED:** Hestonville, Philadelphia. July 1861.

COMMANDER: Col. William Rickards, Jr. (1824-1900).

MONUMENT LOCATIONS: 1) On Culp's Hill about 30 yards northwest of the intersection of South Slocum and Geary Avenues, north of the Pardee field. Represents the regiment's position on the night of July 2nd. 2) On the east shoulder of South Slocum Ave. 40 yards south of Geary Ave. Also on Culp's Hill, this marker represents the position charged to and occupied on July 3rd. **MAP:** VI, D-4/5.

STRENGTH: 10 cos, 357 effectives. **LOSSES:** K-15, W-43, M-8. Total: 66. Percent Loss: 18.5.

WEAPONS: .58 Springfields & .577 Enfields.

SUMMARY: Moved with the brigade into line of battle near the present-day intersection of the Baltimore Pike and the Hospital Road, somewhere below the northeast slope of Powers Hill. On the morning of July 2nd they advanced with the brigade to Culp's Hill, going into position at the site of the No. 2 monument. Built extensive earthworks through most of the day, not engaged. At dusk they moved with the brigade to the left center of the Union line to reinforce the III Corps. Returned to their position on Culp's Hill during the night to find their works occupied by the enemy. Pulled back , with numerous casualties, from their No. 2 monument on South Slocum Ave. to the position of their first monument 100 yards to the north. Lay under arms for the remainder of the night.

UNIT: 111th Infantry. **OTHER NAME:** None.

ORGANIZATION: XII Corps, 2nd Div., 2nd Brig.

RAISED: From the Counties of Crawford, Erie & Warren. **MUSTERED:** Camp Reed, Erie, Jan. 24, 1862.

COMMANDER: Lt. Col. Thomas M. Walker (1834-1910).

MONUMENT LOCATION: Located on Culp's Hill on the east shoulder above South Slocum Ave., directly east of its intersection with Geary Ave. Represents their position for both July 2nd and 3rd. **MAP:** VI, D-5.

STRENGTH: 10 cos, 191 effectives. **LOSSES:** K-5, W-17, M-0, Total: 22. Percent Loss: 11.5.

WEAPONS: .577 Enfields.

SUMMARY: Arrived on the field near Rock Creek in the late afternoon of July 1st. Went into position near the present intersection of the Baltimore Pike and the Hospital Road, northeast of and below Powers Hill. On the morning of July 2nd they advanced with the brigade to Culp's Hill and went into position at the site of their present-day monument. Spent most of the forenoon building earthworks. At dusk they pulled out of their position, and with the brigade moved to the left center of the Union line to reinforce the III Corps. Returned to Culp's Hill well after dark to discover that their position was occupied by the enemy. After a brief fire fight, the regiment pulled back to the stone wall bordering the western edge of the present Pardee Field, and went into position on the north shoulder of Geary Ave. Held this position throughout the night.

Report of Lieut. Col. Thomas M. Walker, One hundred and eleventh Pennsylvania Infantry. LITTLESTOWN, PA., July 6, 1863.

SIR: The regiment in connection with the brigade was moved into line of battle on the right of the Baltimore pike during the forenoon of the 2d instant, the One hundred and ninth Pennsylvania Volunteers on our left, and connections with the First Division on the right. We at once began building a rifle-pit of logs and stone, which was finished in about three hours.

We were undisturbed behind this, and remained until a little before dark, when we were ordered to move to the rear and abandon our works. After marching about a mile to the rear, we were again conducted up the Baltimore pike to occupy our old position. The Twenty-ninth Pennsylvania Volunteers, that preceded us, having been fired on from the position we were to occupy, we halted, and then moved with caution, endeavoring to get back to the trenches.

At about 11 o'clock, having got into the rear of General Greene's brigade, which still occupied their rifle-pits, I was ordered to place my men in the trenches, and proceeded to do so, under the supposition that there was no enemy in our vicinity. Two companies on the left, which were marching in front had been placed in position, when we received a volley from the hill, not over 6 rods from our flank and rear. I immediately placed the remaining companies in line perpendicular to the works and facing the direction of the fire we had received, sent out scouts, and ascertained positively that the hill and works on the right were occupied by the rebels, and reported to Colonel Cobham. I was ordered again by Colonel Cobham to place my men in the rifle-pits, but, protesting that my regiment would then rest so as to be enfiladed by the line of the enemy, he permitted me to retain the position I had selected.

UNIT: 28th Infantry. **OTHER NAME:** None.

ORGANIZATION: XII Corps. 2nd Div., 1st Brig.

RAISED: From the counties of Allegheny, Carbon, Luzerne, Philadelphia, & Westmorland.

MUSTERED: Camp Coleman, Philadelphia, June, 28,1861.

COMMANDER: Capt. John H. Flynn (1819-1875).

MONUMENT LOCATION: 1) (Pictured) On Culp's Hill just off the west shoulder of North Slocum Avenue where the road bends back at left angles to the Federal entrenchments, representing their position on the night of July 2nd and all of July 3rd. 2) Near Rock Creek at the base of east Culp's Hill, 100 yards east of East Confederate Avenue. Represents their forward position on the morning and forenoon of July 2nd. **MAP:** VI, C-5, C-7.

STRENGTH: 9 Cos, (Co. B detached as Provost guard), 303 effectives. **LOSSES:** K-3, W-23, M-2. **Total:** 28. **Percent Loss**: 9.2.

WEAPONS: .58 Springfields & .577 Enfields.

SUMMARY: Moved to South Cemetery Ridge on the evening of July 1st and occupied a position north of the today's intersection of the Wheatfield Road and Sykes Avenue just north of Little Round Top. Skirmishers were sent west through the Wheatfield and Trostle Woods, moving as far west as the Emmitsburg Road, making contact with Buford's cavalry division in rear of the Sherfy Peach Orchard. Moved to Culp's Hill with the brigade at dawn on July 2nd, moving east via the Wheatfield and Granite Schoolhouse Roads,

Hill indicated by their No. 1 monument on North Slocum Ave. Several men wounded during their withdrawal from Rock Creek. Moved with the brigade off Culp's Hill south down the Baltimore Pike to a still unknown bivouac. Returned with the brigade to Culp's Hill at dawn, occupying the position indicated by their No. 1 monument.

Report of Capt. John Flynn, Twenty-eighth Pennsylvania Infantry. GETTYSBURG, PA., July 4, 1863.

LIEUTENANT: Agreeably to orders received from brigade headquarters, on the morning of the 2d, the regiment was thrown to the front along the stream near the right of the line of battle, and remained in that position during the day, supporting the line of skirmishers of General Greene's brigade. Some skirmishing with the enemy, in which 3 men were lost to the command.

Retired at dark with the brigade, and formed line about 1 mile in the rear.

UNIT: 147th Infantry. **OTHER NAME:** None.

ORGANIZATION: XII Corps. 2nd div., 1st Brig.

RAISED: From the counties of Allegheny, Dauphin, Huntingdon, Luzerne, & Philadelphia.

MUSTERED: Harpers Ferry, West Virginia, October, 1862.

COMMANDER: Lt. Col. Ario Pardee, Jr. (1839-1901).

MONUMENT LOCATIONS: 1) At the intersection of Sykes Avenue and the Wheatfield Road on Cemetery Ridge, just north of Little Round Top, representing their first battle line (they were not engaged) on the night of July 1st and early morning of July 2nd. 2) **(pictured)** On the west shoulder of Geary Avenue just opposite the Pardee Field, representing the basic position occupied by the regiment on July 2nd. 3) A simple marker to Co G, located just south of the No. 2 monument. 4) Near the west center of the Pardee Field, approximately 100 yards east of the No. 2 monument, representing the regiment's action on July 3rd. **MAP:** VI, C-4.

STRENGTH: 8 Cos, 298 effectives. **LOSSES:** K-5, W-15, M-0. Total: 20. Percent Loss: 6.7.

WEAPONS: .58 Springfields & .577 Enfields.

SUMMARY: Arrived with the brigade near Rock Creek at approximately 4:00 p.m. on the afternoon of July 1st, via Two Taverns and the Baltimore Pike. Moved west to Cemetery Ridge taking a position to the north of Little Round Top, as indicated by their monument. Formed line of battle in support of one section of the 5th United States Artillery, Battery K. Skirmishers were sent west, moving across the Plum Run Valley and into the Wheatfield and Rose Woods. Reconnoitered as far west as the Emmitsburg Road, making contact with Buford's cavalry in rear of Sherfy's Peach Orchard. Moved to Culp's Hill at dawn on July 2nd with the brigade, possibly without official orders, leaving the Round Tops unsupported. Marched east via the Wheatfield and Granite Schoolhouse Roads, then north on the Baltimore Pike. Went into position a few hundred yards north of their No. 2 monument just off Geary Avenue. Pulled back after dark and moved south down the Baltimore pike to an unidentified position. Spent the rest of the night and early morning in a bivouac off the field of battle. Returned to the position indicated by their No. 2 monument at dawn on July 3rd.

Report of Lieut. Col. Ario Pardee, Jr., One hundred and forty-seventh Pennsylvania Infantry. Near Gettysburg, Pa., July 4, 1863.
Sir: My regiment was relieved from picket duty early on the morning of the 2d, and marched with the brigade to the position on the right of the line occupied by the First Army Corps. In this position we remained until evening, when we marched with the brigade to a position near and east of the turnpike leading from Gettysburg to Baltimore.
On the morning of the 3d, we marched to a point near the line of the previous day and toward the right of the line of the brigade, having on our right the Seventh Regiment Ohio

Volunteers and on our left the Fifth Regiment Ohio Volunteers. Soon after the line was formed, I was ordered by General Geary, commanding division, to move forward with my regiment to a point which commanded the right of the line of intrenchments, and from which a view could be had of the movements of the enemy. My regiment, soon after reaching its assigned position, became engaged with the skirmishers of the enemy, who were soon driven from their position. Skirmishers were sent to the front and right flank, into the woods, from which they greatly harassed the enemy. At about 8 a.m. an attempt was made by the enemy to turn the right of the line of the intrenchments. They boldly advanced to within about 100 yards without discovering my regiment. I then ordered the regiment to fire, and broke their line. They reformed again as a body and advanced. Their advance was checked by the heavy fire they received, when they broke and ran. I would have charged them, but had no support, and would not have been able to have held their position against the column in their rear.

UNIT: 46th Infantry. **OTHER NAME:** None.

ORGANIZATION: XII Corps, 1st Div., 1st Brig.

RAISED: From the Counties of Allegheny, Berks, Dauphin, Luzerne, Mifflin, Northampton, & Potter. **MUSTERED:** Camp Curtin, Harrisburg, Oct. 31, 1861.

COMMANDER: Col. James L. Selfridge (1824-1887).

MONUMENT LOCATION: A few yards above the east shoulder of Slocum Ave., about 100 yards north of its intersection with Geary Ave., on the lower slope of Culps Hill. Represents both July 2nd & 3rd. **MAP:** VI, E-5.

STRENGTH: 10 Cos, 262 effectives. **LOSSES:** K-2, W-10, M-1. Total: 13. Percent Loss: 5.0.

WEAPONS: .58 Springfields.

SUMMARY: At approximately 4:30 p.m. on July 1st the division was moved north, via today's Highland Ave., crossing Rock Creek toward the Hanover Road. The 46th was formed line of battle on east Brinkerhoff's Ridge with skirmishers to the front, facing Benner's Hill one quarter mile to the west. Did not engage. Pulled back to Rock Creek on the repulse of the XI Corps. On the morning of July 2nd the regiment was sent to Culp's Hill where it constructed extensive earthworks throughout the day at the site of their present monument on Slocum Ave. Held this position unengaged until ordered to the left center to support the III Corps. Returned to the position of their monument, to find their works in the hands of the enemy. Took position approximately 200 yards to the west in rear of the stone wall bordering Geary Ave. on the western edge of today's Pardee Field. Several men were wounded during a spirited but futile attempt to drive the enemy out. Remained in the Pardee field sleeping under arms.

Report of Col. James L. Selfridge, Forty-sixth Pennsylvania Infantry. Camp Near Sandy Hook, MD., July 18, 1863.

Sir: On the 2d instant, marched to a position nearer the town and south of it, and to the right of the Gettysburg and Littlestown pike, and, by your orders, commenced making breastworks in great haste, which were completed in the afternoon of the same day, and I immediately guarded the same.

On the same evening, under your command, I was called from the breastworks, and proceeded with other regiments of your brigade to a point near the left of the main line. After a short halt and several hours' absence from the breastworks, I retraced my steps with the intention of reoccupying my late position in the breastworks.

When I approached the breastworks, found the enemy in possession of the same, and, in accordance with your orders, I took up a position in an open field on protecting ground near the breastworks, where I remained until the morning of the 3d, with the men concealed as much as possible from the bullets of the sharpshooters.

At daybreak our artillery opened fire on the enemy, and several batteries in our rear, from an eminence, were obliged to throw their shot and shell immediately over my command,

and from the premature explosions of our shells, and others from our batteries unexploded, falling in the midst of my command.

During the day my command was much annoyed by sharpshooters, but I suffered no loss of life or injury in my command from the same.

2ND CITATION, JULY 2ND & 3rd: 74th Infantry. [Note: Main monument missing. Included is a photo of their right flank marker].

GENERAL INFORMATION & DATA: See 74th Infantry, July 1st.

MONUMENT LOCATION: Right flank marker is inside the National Cemetery above the Taneytown Road. Represents the position occupied on July 2nd and 3rd. **Map:** VII, B-2.

SUMMARY: Held this position in rear of a stone wall once located in the vicinity of today's flank markers in the National Cemetery above the Taneytown Road. Held in reserve supporting the numerous batteries posted to their immediate rear. Skirmishers posted west of the Emmitsburg Road were kept active by a continuous steady engagement with the enemy posted east of today's Long Lane. Several men wounded by artillery fire on July 2nd, with two killed by sharpshooters posted in the buildings south of town. Held this position throughout July 3rd, not engaged but subjected to a continuous artillery crossfire that pummeled their position. Three men killed on July 3rd, two by sharpshooters, one vaporized by an exploding shell. Held their position until July 5th. One detail was sent into town on the evening of July 4th in search of information about the regiment's missing casualties from the battle of July 1st. Helped to bury Federal dead throughout Cemetery Hill and

Ridge.

2ND CITATION, JULY 2ND & 3rd: 75th Infantry.

GENERAL INFORMATION & DATA: See 75th Infantry, July 1st.

MONUMENT LOCATION: In the National Cemetery west of the Baltimore Pike near the statue of General Reynolds. Represents the position occupied on July 2nd & 3rd.

SUMMARY: Held their position approximately 50 yards northwest of their present monument, in rear of a low stone wall on the brow of Cemetery Hill. Skirmishers posted at various points about the fields and lots southeast of the Dobbin House were in constant battle with enemy sharpshooters and riflemen in nearby buildings and lots. Subjected to continuous enemy rifle fire. Several men hit by sharpshooters, none killed. Held this position throughout July 3rd, not engaged. Several men wounded, one mortally, during the great cannonade and by the continuous small-arms fire. Held this position until July 5th. Reconnoitering details were sent into town and on toward the battlefield of July 1st in search of missing and wounded.

July 3rd

Guide To Pennsylvania Troops

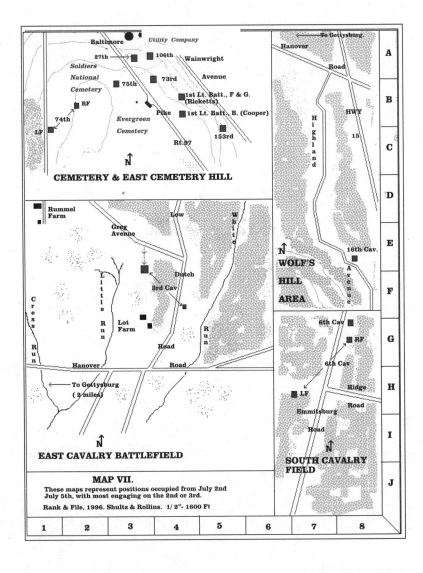

CEMETERY & EAST CEMETERY HILL

Baltimore
Utility Company
27th
106th
Wainwright
Soldiers
National
Cemetery
73rd
Avenue
75th
1st Lt. Batt., F & G. (Ricketts)
RF
Pike
1st Lt. Batt. B. (Cooper)
74th
Evergreen
Cemetery
LF
153rd
Rt.97
N

EAST CAVALRY BATTLEFIELD

Rummel Farm
Low
White
Greg Avenne
Little Run
Dutch
3rd Cav
Cress Run
Lot Farm
Run Run
Road
Run
Hanover
Road
To Gettysburg
(2 miles)
N

WOLF'S HILL AREA

To Gettysburg
Hanover
Road
Highland
HWY
15
16th Cav.
N
Avenue

SOUTH CAVALRY FIELD

6th Cav
RF
6th Cav
Ridge
LF
Road
Emmitsburg
Road
Road
N

MAP VII.

These maps represent positions occupied from July 2nd
July 5th, with most engaging on the 2nd or 3rd.

Rank & File, 1996. Shultz & Rollins. 1/2"- 1600 Ft

A B C D E F G H I J
1 2 3 4 5 6 7 8

July 3rd.

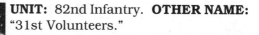

UNIT: 82nd Infantry. **OTHER NAME:** "31st Volunteers."

ORGANIZATION: VI Corps, 3rd Div., 1st Brig.

RAISED: From the Counties of Crawford, Erie, amd Forest.
MUSTERED: Camp McLane, Erie. Sept, 8, 1861

COMMANDER: Capt. Orpheus P. Woodward (1835-1919).

MONUMENT LOCATION: On the west shoulder of North Slocum Avenue, approximately 100 yards north of its intersection with Williams Avenue on Culp's Hill. **MAP:** VI, C-4. .

STRENGTH: 10 Cos, 320 effectives. **LOSSES:** K-0, W-6, M-0. Total: 6. Percent loss: 2.2

WEAPONS: .577 Enfields.

SUMMARY: Arrived on the field late in the afternoon of July 2nd. Held in reserve near the Baltimore Pike and Rock Creek. Near midnight the regiment was detached from Shaler's brigade and sent to the Taneytown Road where it rested in reserve until the midmorning of July 3rd. Marched to Culp's Hill via the Tanytown Road and the Baltimore Pike, arriving near noon. The regiment was re-attached to Shaler's VI Corps brigade and placed in rear of the front line of the fortifications on Culp's Hill. Relieved the 122nd New York Infantry in the entrenchments upon the Confederate repulse. Moved over the works taking prisoners. Recalled to Cemetery Ridge with the brigade in the late afternoon, the 82nd moved in rear of McGilvery's artillery line in reserve. Held this position until 4;00 a.m. on the 4th. Moved back toward Rock Creek where it was posted in reserve until July 5th. Details formed to bury dead and collect arms.

2ND CITATION, JULY 3RD: 111th Infantry.

GENERAL INFORMATION & DATA: See July 2.

MONUMENT LOCATION: See July 2nd. **MAP:** VI, D-5.

SUMMARY: Began to fire at enemy skirmishers moving in the dark toward their line in the woods in rear of today's Pardee Field. Held their position firing at enfilade into the entrenched Confederate line, driving all their skirmishers back. Fought nearly eight hours from this position, eventually driving the enemy force back and recapturing their entrenchments. Temporarily relieved, the 111th moved back into these works and held them until July 5th. Detailed to bury dead on the 4th.

Report. We remained in this position watching the enemy until 3 a.m., when it was determined the line should be changed a very little to the rear, so as to get the advantage of a wing of General Greene's trenches. I was endeavoring to move my regiment, a man at a time, with the utmost caution, when our watchful enemy detected a move, and, supposing we were about to retire, opened fire upon us. My men returned the fire, silencing theirs, and then moved to the position assigned them, awaiting daylight for the work to begin.

Picket firing began with the first streak of light, and about 3:45 o'clock the line of the enemy advanced with a yell. We opened fire briskly, quickly compelling them to take the shelter of the rocks and of our own trenches that were in their possession.

We continued fighting in this way until 5:55 o'clock, when we were relieved by the Twenty-ninth Regiment Pennsylvania Volunteers for the purpose of renewing our ammunition. After filling our boxes and wiping our guns, we returned to the same position, and continued the fight until we had again exhausted our ammunition, and were in turn relieved by the Twenty-ninth Pennsylvania Volunteers. Soon after this, about 1 o'clock, the enemy retired, giving up the contest.

In this fight, about half of my regiment was in open

July 3rd.

line, fighting a desperate enemy behind the very rifle-pits they had built for their own protection. I am proud to say they fought feeling they were Pennsylvanians in Pennsylvania. We expended 160 rounds to the man.

I wish to mention as deserving praise for great bravery and coolness, Captains Woeltge, Thomas, and Warner; also that Sergeants [Henry] Dieffenbach, [George] Selkregg, [Andrew W.] Tracy, [Andrew J.] Bemis, [John L.] Wells, and [Mills F.] Allison, and privates John Hughes and Orrin Sweet deserve mention.

2ND CITATION, JULY 3RD: 109th Infantry.

GENERAL INFORMATION & DATA: See July 2.

MONUMENT LOCATION: See July 2nd. **MAP:** VI, C-5.

SUMMARY: Near dawn on the 3rd, the regiment opened a brisk musketry fire from their position in the Pardee field toward the entrenched Confederates who occupied the rifle pits previously constructed by the 109th on July 2nd. Fought nearly eight hours non-stop, eventually driving the rebels out from their captured Federal works indicated by the position of their monument. Held this position until July 5th. Details were formed to bury dead and collect and destroy captured and disabled weapons.

Report: Toward morning we retired some 25 paces behind rocks, being an admirable protection from the enemy's fire and at the same time a very advantageous position to do execution.

At 4 o'clock on the morning of the 3d, the firing commenced immediately in our front, we occupying the right of the brigade. From occasional shots the firing soon became regular, being handsomely replied to by us. A constant fire of musketry was kept up. We assisted in successfully repelling a charge of the enemy, causing terrible slaughter, throwing them into confusion, and putting them to flight.

At 10. 30 a.m. we were relieved by a regiment of the First Division, Sixth Corps, having been in action six consecutive hours. We merely retired to the rear some 300 yards.

We remained here until 2:30 p.m., when we were ordered again to the woods to hold the fortifications—those that the enemy held till the morning—our original position. While here we were exposed to an artillery fire with occasional musketry in our front, which lasted at intervals during the night, ceasing as the morning dawned.

Both officers and men did their duty. Our conduct we prefer others to speak and judge of rather than ourselves. Twice during the engagement our color-bearers were shot down, killing 1 instantly and wounding the other.

2ND CITATION, JULY 3RD: 28th Infantry.

GENERAL INFORMATION & DATA: See July 2.

MONUMENT LOCATION: See July 2. **MAP:** VI, C-4.

SUMMARY: Returned to Culp's Hill on the morning of July 3rd. Heavily engaged within their fortified entrenchments located east of today's Slocum Avenue from their No. 1 monument. Relieved several times during the morning, moving back to the position of their No. 1 monument in rear of the main firing line. Exchanged places throughout the morning with the 29th Ohio, giving the men from both regiments ample time to rest from the continuous small arms fire. Held in rear of the works on the Confederate retreat. Held position until July 5th. Details formed to bury dead and destroy captured and disabled weapons. Pickets established along Rock Creek near the site of their No. 2 monument.

Report: Remained in that position until 12.30 a.m. July 3, when the regiment moved forward to retake the position left the morning before. Took position in the breastworks, relieving the Twenty-ninth Ohio Volunteers. Were under heavy fire while there, and lost during the engagement 3 killed and 22 wounded and missing.

Were relieved, and rested in rear of the brigade until nearly 4 p.m., when we were again ordered into the breastworks, and remained there until 10 p.m.

July 3rd.

I take pleasure in stating that officers and men, without exceptions, exhibited the greatest coolness and bravery, and I would consider it injustice to the command did I attempt to single out individual cases of bravery, as all performed well their part.

UNIT: 23rd Infantry. **OTHER NAME:** "Birney's Zouaves."

ORGANIZATION: VI Corps, 3rd Div., 1st Brig.

RAISED: Philadelphia City. **MUSTERED:** Philadelphia. Aug. 2, 1862.

COMMANDER: Lt. Col. John F. Glenn (1829-1905).

MONUMENT LOCATION: Located on the west shoulder of South Slocum avenue, 75 yards north of its intersection with Geary Avenue, Culps hill. **MAP:** VI, C-4.

STRENGTH: 10 Cos, 467 effectives. **LOSSES:** K-1, W-13, M-0. Total: 13. Percent Loss: 3.0

WEAPONS: .54 Austrians.

SUMMARY: Arrived on the field of battle late in the afternoon of July 2nd. Placed in reserve throughout the night in a position opposite Rock Creek just off the Baltimore Pike. At 7:00 a.m. on the 3rd, the regiment reported with the brigade, less the 82nd Pa., to Culp's Hill for assignment as the battle was raging. Moving into a reserve position in rear of the front fortifications, the 23rd remained unengaged for some two hours before being called forward. As ordered. Only five companies from its ten were ordered forward. These five companies moved into the breastworks, clearly visible today, 40 yards east of their monument. Fought for one hour, becoming heavily engaged. Charged over the works and down toward the base of Culp's Hill as the Confederates pulled back. At approximately 11:30 a.m., the balance of the regiment moved forward to support the wing already engaged. Pulled out of line of battle and sent to Cemetery Ridge where they went into a reserve position in rear of McGilvery's line. Held this position until July 4th when the regiment was pulled back to the Baltimore Pike and placed in reserve. Details formed to bury dead and collect arms.

2ND CITATION, JULY 3RD: 147th Infantry.

GENERAL INFORMATION & DATA: See July 2.

MONUMENT LOCATION: See July 2nd. **MAP:** VI, D-4.

SUMMARY: Arrived back on Culp's Hill sometime well after the fighting had opened. Laid in reserve in the woods northwest of the Pardee field. Advanced to the Pardee Field, to the position of their No. 1 monument, driving the enemy beyond. Held position in rear of a stonewall as the enemy attempted to again cross the field in mass. Fired several near point-blank volleys into the enemy lines which broke and fled the field in disorder. Remained at the position of their No. 2 monument engaging the enemy across the field for several hours. After the Confederate retreat from Culp's Hill, the regiment was moved to a position in rear of Cutler's I Corps brigade. Held this unmarked position until July 5th. Helped in the burial of dead throughout Culp's Hill, especially in the Pardee field.

3rd CITATION, JULY 3RD: 56th Infantry.

GENERAL INFORMATION & DATA: See July 2.

MONUMENT LOCATION: None (Marker on Culp's Hill missing). **MAP:** VI, A-5.

SUMMARY: From their position atop Culp's Hill, anchoring the right flank of Cutler's I Corps brigade, the 56th lent little

July 3rd.

support to the XII Corps regiments on their immediate right. With the hill too precipitous for Confederates to scale in front of the regiment's entrenchments, the 56th was left unmolested in a reserve position. Men from the right companies were engaged but did little damage. At about 3:00 p.m. the 56th, along with the 7th Indiana and 95th New York, pulled out of line and marched toward the Copse of Trees on Cemetery Ridge. Arrived near the Angle on Pickett's repulse and was immediately put in a reserve position somewhere near Army Headquarters. Did not engage. Held this until the morning of July 4th when they returned to Culp's Hill. A detail sent toward Rock Creek bagged several enemy prisoners including one major. Held their position atop Culp's Hill until July 5th. Details helped bury the dead on Culp's Hill as well as destroy captured and disabled arms.

2ND CITATION, JULY 3RD: 46th infantry.

GENERAL INFORMATION & DATA: See July 2.

MONUMENT LOCATION: See July 2nd.
MAP: VI, E-5.

SUMMARY: Held their position in today's Pardee Field adjacent to their captured breastworks. At dawn they were hit by friendly artillery fire from Federal batteries posted on the Baltimore Pike, which caused several casualties. Held in reserve with little or no action, except for sharpshooting and skirmishing. After the Confederate retreat from Culp's Hill at about 12:30 p.m., the 46th retook possession of their breastworks. Near 3:00 p.m. moved toward the Copse of Trees with the 123rd New York. The 123rd continued over Cemetery Ridge to engage Pickett's retreating columns, while the 46th was stopped and placed in line of battle just west of Army Headquarters. Many men from the 46th broke ranks and wandered over the ridge toward the Angle and Copse of Trees in time to see Confederate infantry still visible in the fields west of the Emmitsburg

Road. At about 5:00 p.m. returned to Culp's Hill where it held its position at its present monument until July 5th. Helped bury Confederate dead in one large mass grave in the Pardee Field. On July 5th Col. Selfridge attempted, with no success, to find out which battery was responsible for the casualties in his regiment.

2ND CITATION, JULY 3RD: 29th Infantry.

GENERAL INFORMATION & DATA: See July 2.

MONUMENT LOCATION: See July 2nd. **MAP:** VI, D3/4.

SUMMARY: Held a position throughout the night of July 2nd approximately 100 yards northeast of their present monument. Charged and drove the Rebels from their entrenchments at the site of their present day monument. Fought without a break for nearly eight hours. Held this position until July 5th. Skirmishers were sent east of the Rock Creek to reconnointer, as well as details formed to bury dead and collect arms.

2ND CITATION, JULY 3RD: 1st Light, Batteries F & G Consolidated. (Ricketts)

GENERAL INFORMATION & DATA: See July 2.

MONUMENT LOCATION: See July 2nd. **MAP:** VII, B-4.

SUMMARY: Held East Cemetery Hill position throughout July 3rd, less one gun disabled on July 2nd. Opened at first light firing at supposed enemy batteries near Benner's Hill. Ordered to cease fire by Brig. Gen. H. J. Hunt as results from fire could not be seen. Sat unengaged through all the forenoon and early afternoon while exposed to a severe left enfilade cross-fire from expert enemy marksmen and sharpshooters at the south end of town. Fired at enemy batteries on Benner's Hill during the great cannonade doing good execution. Continued to hold position throughout the

July 3rd.

cannonade up to Pickett's advance. As ordered, Captain Ricketts led one section (two guns) west across the Baltimore Pike, and into the Evergreen Cemetery. From a position on southwest Cemetery Hill, Ricketts' section fired into Pickett's attacking columns with excellent results. Their field of fire would have been east over today's Cyclorama building toward the Codori farm and Emmitsburg Road. Ricketts was reinforced by one other section on the repulse, but did not engage. Returned to their position on East cemetery Hill indicated by their monument until July 5th.

2ND CITATION, JULY 3RD: 3rd Heavy Artillery, Battery H. (Rank, one section)

GENERAL INFORMATION & DATA: See July 2.

MONUMENT LOCATION: Plaque and marker for July 3rd in McGilvery's artillery line, Hancock Avenue, south Cemetery Ridge. **MAP:** V, H-5.

SUMMARY: Arrived at this position at approximately 7:00 a.m. on July 3rd from the Artillery Reserve Park. Dug in on the brow of south Cemetery Ridge, approximately 40 yards southwest of their marker. Sat unengaged for most of the day, allowing the great cannonade to pass overhead. As ordered, returned fire slowly and deliberately. Opened with good effect on Pickett's right flank infantry brigade (Kemper) as soon as it emerged from the swales 1,600 yards to the front. Helped in the repulse of Pickett's Charge by firing 175 rounds of ammunition in less than one hour. Continued after the Charge to engage in counter-battery fire with enemy batteries. Held this position until July 5th,

3rd CITATION, JULY 3RD: 151st infantry.

GENERAL INFORMATION & DATA: July 2.

MONUMENT LOCATION: None. **MAP:** V, E-6.

SUMMARY: Held position to the immediate left of the

present monument dedicated to the 80th New York Volunteer Infantry on Cemetery Ridge, approximately 300 yards south of the Copse of Trees, throughout the great cannonade and the beginning of Pickett's Charge. Fired volleys into the right flank of Kemper's brigade as it moved due north in front of the regiment. Pulled out of line following Kemper's line north. Many men were mixed up with troops from the 150th, 143rd, and 149th regiments as they moved forward and north from a reserve position just in rear of the 151st. Men from the 151st helped recapture the guns belonging to the 1st New York Battery B as they approached the overrun section from the south. Many men continued on to finish the battle at or near the Copse of Trees. Returned to previous position and reorganized. Held this position until July 5th. Men detailed to bury dead and destroy captured and disabled arms. One detail sent into town and on to Seminary Ridge for information about their missing casualties from the battle on July 1st.

2ND CITATION, JULY 3RD: 69th Infantry.

GENERAL INFORMATION & DATA: See July 2.

MONUMENT LOCATION: See July 2nd. **MAP:** V, C-5.

SUMMARY: Occupied the low stonewall west of the Copse of Trees throughout the morning while taking artillery fire. Held this position into the afternoon and through the great cannonade. This part of the Federal line was the focal point of the massed enemy batteries posted to the west, not to mention the spot that Longstreet's attack was to guide on. Accepted Pickett's massed columns as they moved slowly east over the Emmitsburg Road. Partially overrun and forced back from the wall, the 69th fought on in vicious hand-to-hand combat for 15 minutes with superior enemy numbers as Federal reinforcements converged on their position. Bent back at right angles to the wall, the right companies delivered crippling volleys into Armistead's attacking few who crossed over the wall at the Angle. Took heavy casualties. Held this position until July 5th. Buried

July 3rd.

dead at the Angle, Copse of Trees, and Codori farm.

Report: The battle commenced on the 3d instant at about 4 p.m. We still held the position assigned us the day previous. At about 1 o'clock a most fierce cannonading took place, and was continued without intermission till about 3 o'clock, when the rebels advanced a large infantry force against our whole line. Onward they came, and it would seem as if no power could hold them in check. Our troops, with few exceptions, met them bravely, but still they came, and, as they advanced to the right of our regiment, turned by the right flank and literally came right on top of our men. But if they succeeded thus far in their advance, they were here held in check, for new ardor seemed to inspire our men to greater exertions. Our whole brigade here became engaged with them, and, with the help of the Tammany Regiment and the Twentieth Massachusetts Regiment, drove them from the front of our line. We lost very heavily, and among the number killed we have to deplore our colonel, D. O'Kane, and lieutenant-colonel, M. Tschudy. Our major was also wounded at this juncture, and the command fell into my hands. After the enemy had been completely driven back, I put our men to work to still further strengthen our position in the event of any other advance on the part of the enemy on the following day. Our killed were all buried together, and their graves marked, so that their friends and connections can easily find them if they wish to have them disinterred. The wounded were taken to hospitals temporarily erected, and cared for as well as circumstances would admit.

2ND CITATION, JULY 3RD: 71st Infantry.

GENERAL INFORMATION & DATA: See July 2.

MONUMENT LOCATION: See July 2nd. **MAP:** V, B-5.

SUMMARY: Upon reaching a position in rear of Cushing's 4th U.S. Artillery, Battery A., near midnight on the 2nd, the 71st retook their previous position in support of the battery by moving to its right behind the stonewall at the inner ngle and to its left in rear of the Copse of Trees. Several of its companies were posted behind the stone wall in front of Cushing's battery, at the position indicated by their monument at the Angle. Held this position throughout the morning under enemy artillery fire. Most of the regiment was posted either behind the stonewall on the brow of the ridge, to the left of Arnold's Rhode Island battery, or the forward wall at the Angle by the monument. Held this position throughout the great cannonade, many men from the 71st replacing Cushing's casualties as they occurred. Accepted Pickett's attack from the Angle, being overrun at the forward wall and pushed back through Cushing's wrecked battery. With the regiment split up, its men fought in mass with other Federal units that converged on the Angle. Countercharged to the forward stonewall capturing many prisoners and several enemy colors. Held this position throughout the evening, pulling back to the crest after midnight to their original position in rear of the Copse of Trees. Held this position until July 5th. Helped in the burying of dead and collecting of arms.

Report: On the 3d instant, some 50 of my men assisted in working Lieutenant Cushing's battery, while the balance were in position, protected by a stone wall from an infantry attack, engaging the enemy and scattering confusion in his ranks, taking some 500 prisoners, as many arms, and 3 stand of rebel colors.* Among so many conspicuous acts of valor and daring, it is difficult to particularize individuals. I cannot but speak of my regiment in the highest terms. I would call attention to the conduct of Captain McMahon and Private Young, of Company C, both of whom are under sentence of court-martial. I pray that the approval or disapproval of the findings of the court in the case of the first may be influenced in a great degree by his noble conduct in the field, and of the latter that the sentence may be revoked.

* A medal of honor awarded to Private John E. Clopp for the capture of the flag of the Ninth Virginia Infantry.

2ND CITATION, JULY 3RD : 106th Infantry.

GENERAL INFORMATION & DATA: See July 2.

July 3rd.

MONUMENT LOCATION: Ssee July 2nd. **MAP:** V, C-5.

SUMMARY: Regiment divided into two sections. 1) Companies A and B laid in reserve in rear of the Copse of Trees as indicated by monument No. 1, supporting Perrin's 1st Rhode Island Light Artillery, Battery B (Brown) throughout the morning and most of the great cannonade. With permission, the demi-regiment was allowed to move forward through the thickets to a safer position in rear of the stonewall on the left of the 69th Pa. During Pickett's Charge the regiment was pulled back in order to make room for a fresh battery (Cowan's) and reformed their small line of battle to immediate north of said battery. Held their ground in mass with reinforcements, counter-charging in two directions on the repulse. The right wing moved due north toward the Angle, while the left wing moved back through the thickets to the stone wall. Captured many prisoners. 2) With companies A and B detached on Cemetery Ridge, the balance of the regiment held their position in rear of the stonewall on the northern crest of East Cemetery Hill at the position indicated by the No. 2 monument. Several volunteer details were sent forward toward the town before dawn, acting as sharpshooters and skirmishers. Helped to silence the enemy riflemen who were creating havoc for the Federal gunners atop Cemetery Hill. Held this position until July 4th when the 11th Corps regiments on their line moved forward in mass and into town. The 106th returned to Webb's brigade on Cemetery Ridge where it helped bury the dead in the angle. Held this position until July 5th. Details formed to bury dead and collect arms.

2ND CITATION, JULY 3RD: 72nd Infantry.

GENERAL INFORMATION & DATA: See July 2.

MONUMENT LOCATION: See July 2nd. **MAP:** V, B-5.

SUMMARY FOR JULY 3RD: Lay in line of battle near the top of Cemetery Ridge approximately one hundred yards east of their present monument in rear and in support of Cushing's battery. Exposed to a deadly and accurate Confederate cross-fire during the great cannonade. Eight men killed with twice as many wounded while on this line. Approximately two dozen men were detached, as volunteers, to help man Cushing's wrecked battery. Moved forward to the west brow of Cemetery Ridge in rear of the Copse of Trees during Pickett's assualt and held their ground. Extreme casualties taken at this position as the enemy had the 72nd line silhouetted against the eastern sky. Charged to the wall on the repulse helping drive Pickett's columns back toward the Emmitsburg Road. Many prisoners and enemy colors taken. Held this position until July 5th. Detailed to bury the Confederate dead at the Angle, the men of the 72nd simply dug 18-inch-deep trenches and dumped the bodies in, covering them with a few inches of dirt. Helped in the burying of dead and collecting of arms. Survivors were denied request to erect a monument at wall by Monument Commission, which argued that they refused to charge forward to the wall. Pennsylvania Supreme Court found in favor of the regiment.

Report: On the 3d instant, the regiment was again assigned the duty of supporting a battery, which position it occupied (under a terrific fire of the enemy's artillery) until 3 p.m., at which time they were ordered to advance upon the stone wall on our immediate front, it being discovered that the enemy were making a demonstration in that direction. At this point the regiment became engaged with Pickett's division of the rebel army, and, after a severe contest, lasting about half an hour, succeeded in routing the enemy and occupying the wall, which position it held until the withdrawal of the brigade on the morning of the 5th. In this engagement the regiment captured two rebel colors and a number of prisoners. I would especially mention Companies A and I, Captains Suplee and Cook, for the creditable manner in which they performed the skirmishing for the brigade in the engagements of both days.

July 3rd.

2ND CITATION, JULY 3RD: 99th Infantry.

GENERAL INFORMATION & DATA: See July 2.

MONUMENT LOCATION: On the east shoulder of Hancock Avenue directly east of the Angle, Cemetery Ridge. **MAP:** V, B-5.

SUMMARY: Moved to position indicated by their monument early in the afternoon, possibly during the cannonade. Lay in line of battle to the rear of the 72nd Pa. Infantry. Fought in Webb's line next to the 72nd during Pickett's Charge. When asked to help remove the disabled guns of a battery, Maj. Moore detailed a few men and helped remove three guns. Held position until the morning of July 4th when the regiment was ordered forward to the picket line. Moved south on the 5th and rejoined De Trobriand's III Corps brigade near the Wheatfield. Helped bury their dead from the battle of July 2nd

Report of Maj. John W. Moore, Ninety-ninth Pennsylvania Infantry. NEAR WARRENTON, VA., July 27, 1863.

SIR: Early on the morning of the 3d, I moved my regiment with the brigade to the woods, near the ground occupied by us on the morning of the 2d instant. I remained here until about 1 o'clock, when I moved my regiment, with the Third and Fourth Maine and Twentieth Indiana, of our brigade, under command of Colonel Lakeman, of Third Maine, where I took position on the right of the left center, and reported to General Webb, who commanded the Second Brigade, Second Division, Second Army Corps.

Here the fighting just previous to our arrival had been terrible. My regiment held the front line, when a lieutenant of Battery A, Fourth U. S. Artillery, asked me to draw his pieces to the rear, to prevent them falling into the hands of the enemy, he having only 6 men and 3 horses left that were not disabled. The request was promptly complied with, and the battery removed to the rear, under cover of a hill. Later in the day, another battery was placed in the position of the one removed by my regiment.

In closing my report, it affords me no small degree of pleasure to be able to say that all of my command behaved nobly, standing unmoved under the enemy's fire and resisting superior numbers with spirit and determination. I cannot speak too highly of the manner in which the officers of my command acted, without exception gallantly and efficiently performing every duty assigned them.

I lament to say that First Lieut. John R. Nice, commanding Company H, a brave, efficient, and gallant officer, was mortally wounded in the action of the 2d, and died a few hours afterward. Three other officers were wounded and 102 enlisted men reported killed, wounded, and missing, whose names have been reported in the list of casualties.

The courageous conduct of Color Sergt. Harvey M. Munsell, and the manner in which he bore the regimental colors during the conflict, has induced me to make special mention of his case as one worthy of the most decided approval.

2ND CITATION, JULY 3RD: 114th Infantry.

GENERAL INFORMATION & DATA: See July 2.

MONUMENT LOCATION: On the east shoulder of Hancock Avenue, directly east of the Copse of Trees on Cemetery Ridge. **MAP:** V, B-6.

SUMMARY: Moved north from in rear of McGilvery's artillery line to a position in support of Cowan's 1st New York

July 3rd.

Ind. Battery's first position atop Cemetery Ridge, at a position just north of today's Pleasonton Avenue. Held this reserve position until Cowan moved north to the Copse of Trees. Following Cowan, the 114th detached themselves from the other regiments of Tippen's (Graham's) III Corps brigade, and moved north to lend support as ordered. Reformed their line of battle in rear of Cowan near a position indicated by their monument for July 3rd. Assisted in the repulse of Pickett's Charge. Moved south to the position of the Vermont Brigade and rejoined its brigade after relieving the Vermont regiments on the front line. Held this position for the remainder of the battle. Detailed to help bury the dead.

Report of Capt. Edward R. Bowen, One hundred and fourteenth Pennsylvania Infantry. Fox's GAP, SOUTH MOUNTAIN, MD., July 12, 1863.

SIR: I remained where I was until early daylight of the 3d, when I rejoined the brigade, and we lay all the morning of the 3d in the woods, where we were supplied with rations, and remained until about 3 p.m., when I was ordered to move up to the right by the double-quick, being detached from the brigade to support Cowan's (First New York) battery.

At this time, Colonel Madill, of the One hundred and forty-first Pennsylvania Volunteers, assumed command of the brigade, and I took command of his regiment and my own.

At about 7 p.m. I was ordered to get ready to be relieved, and to send to the front a detail to collect the arms which had been left there. We collected about 300 pieces.

While falling back from the brick house onto the road, and very hotly pressed by the enemy, I saw Lieutenant-Colonel Cavada, who was then commanding the regiment, stopping at a log house in an orchard on our right. I inquired if he was wounded; he replied that he was not, but utterly exhausted. I begged him to make an effort to come on, as the enemy were only a few yards from him and advancing rapidly. He replied that he could not, and I left him there, and not having heard from him since, I have no doubt he was taken prisoner there. I assumed command of the regiment at this time.

I also report a number of men as missing whom I have no doubt were killed and their bodies burned when the barn was burned down, and some, I have no doubt, were taken prisoners at the brick house, among them 2 second lieutenants.

In closing this report, I beg leave to ask that it may be remembered that I was not in command of the regiment until after Lieutenant-Colonel Cavada's capture, and that consequently the report of all that precedes is compiled solely from my own observations and memory.

It affords me great pleasure to testify to the great gallantry and cool courage of Brigadier-General Graham, commanding the First Brigade, First Division, Third Corps, of which my regiment is a part, and to express my regret, in which I am joined by all the officers in my regiment, at his having been wounded, and trust that, his wound proving slight, he will soon return to again lead us to victory.

I am also happy to be able to mention Captains [Francis] Fix and Eddy, the former of whom received a painful wound, and also Lieutenants Robinson, Newlin, and A. W. Fix, for their bravery and efficient assistance during the engagement.

2ND CITATION, JULY 3RD: 141st Infantry.

GENERAL INFORMATION & DATA: See July 2.

MONUMENT LOCATION: None.

SUMMARY: Followed the 114th regiment north in support of Cowan. Reported to Webb who placed them in reserve atop the ridge in rear of the 114th, again possibly supporting either Fitzhugh or Burton. Held their position in support of a battery, some men moved forward and in mass with federal reinforcements helped in the repulse of Pickett's Charge. Near midnight the 141st moved south 300 yards and rejoined the brigade, relieving Stannard's Vermont Brigade at their works. Held this position for the remainder of the battle. Detailed to help bury the dead.

July 3rd.

3rd CITATION, JULY 3RD: 121st infantry.

GENERAL INFORMATION & DATA: See July 2.

MONUMENT LOCATION: See July 2nd. **MAP IV.**

SUMMARY: Laid in reserve near the position of their monument throughout the cannonade. Detached from the brigade as Pickett's columns appeared, moving north toward the Copse of Trees. Moved to a position approximately 75 yards to the southeast in rear of the Copse of Trees, 100 yards north of their monument and formed line of battle in rear of a stone wall atop the crest of Cemetery Ridge. Advanced into the Copse of Trees as the Confederate columns breached the Angle area. Fought in mass helping repulse Pickett's Charge and the Confederate threat on the 2nd Corps line. Returned to the area of their monument after the charge was beaten back.

3rd CITATION, JULY 3RD: 143rd infantry.

GENERAL INFORMATION & DATA: See July 2.

MONUMENT LOCATION: See July 2nd. **MAP:** V, E-5.

SUMMARY: Laid in rear of the Vermont Brigade throughout the morning and halfway through the great cannonade, when a bursting shell in the regiment caused several casualties. The regiment was then allowed to move forward to occupy the position indicated by their present monument. Accepted Pickett's Charge in mass with other Federal regiments. Some of the men moved north toward the Copse of Trees, but most of the regiment held its ground in support of Wheeler's New York battery which squeezed into line somewhere near the 143rd's left flank. Held this position until July 5th. Details formed to help bury dead and collect arms.

3rd CITATION, JULY 3RD: 150th Infantry.

Guide To Pennsylvania Troops

GENERAL INFORMATION & DATA: See July 2.

MONUMENT LOCATION: See July 2nd. **MAP:** V, D-5.

SUMMARY: Held the position indicated by their monument during the cannonade and the beginning of Pickett's Charge. Moved north following Kemper's brigade as it passed in front of the main Federal line. Fired volleys at point-blank range into the right flank of Kemper's right regiment causing heavy casualties. Most of the 150th continued north toward the Copse of Trees until it came to the 1st New York Light Artillery, Battery B which was involved in desperate hand to hand combat just south of the thickets. The 150th reformed their line and assisted in checking the enemy onslaught at that point, and helped resecure Battery B. Many men from the 150th continued on toward the Copse of Trees in small, unorganized groups and as individuals, finishing the battle near the Angle. Returned after the battle to the line indicated by their monument. Held in line during the 4th, assisted in burial details on the 5th.

2ND CITATION, JULY 3RD 57th Infantry.

GENERAL INFORMATION & DATA: See July 2.

MONUMENT LOCATION: None. **MAP:** Not applicable.

SUMMARY: Detached from Ward's brigade in rear of McGilvery's line, the regiment moved north toward the Copse of Trees engaging Pickett's right flank as it, too, moved north. Their probable position was somewhere around today's Vermont Brigade monument. Detailed to support one of General Doubleday's supporting batteries. On the repulse the regiment collected prisoners and arms. Moved back to the George Weikert woods on July 4th, holding that position until July 5th. Helped in burying the dead and collecting of arms.

Report of Capt. Alanson H. Nelson, Fifty-seventh Pennsylvania Infantry, First Brigade. CAMP IN THE FIELD, July 10, 1863.
SIR: We finally reformed in the rear, near the

July 3rd.

Baltimore pike and a large yellow barn, where we remained until 8 a.m. of the next day (3d instant), when we were ordered to the front as a reserve. About 3 p.m. on the 3d instant, we were ordered forward with the brigade to support a battery in General Doubleday's division, First Corps, where we remained until dark; then moved to the front, and acted as a picket reserve until the morning of the 4th instant, when we moved to the left and in rear of a line of breastworks, where we remained until ordered on the present march. All in the command acted well and fought bravely, and where all acted so well it was impossible for one to distinguish himself more than another.

SECOND CITATION, JULY 3RD: 145th Infantry.

GENERAL INFORMATION & DATA: See July 2.

MONUMENT LOCATION: None. **MAP:** Not Applicable.

SUMMARY: Held in reserve in rear of McGilvery's line on Cemetery Ridge. Moved forward during Pickett's Charge in support of McGilvery's artillery line. Collected prisoners and tended to the enemy wounded. After Pickett's repulse, skirmishers were sent forward toward the Emmitsburg Road. Traded shots with a few remaining Confederates holding out at the Abram Trostle farm, driving them across the Emmitsburg Road. One wounded casualty reported. Held position on Cemetery Ridge until July 5th when the regiment was detailed to bury the dead.

Report On Friday, the regiment built a line of intrenchments just in front of its position occupied on Thursday, and lay there all day, subject to a severe fire from the enemy's artillery for several hours. At 4 p.m. a detail for picket was sent to the front and deployed as skirmishers; 1 man was wounded.

2ND CITATION, JULY 3RD: 140th Infantry.

GENERAL INFORMATION & DATA: See July 2.

Guide To Pennsylvania Troops

MONUMENT LOCATION: None. **MAP:** Not applicable.

SUMMARY: Placed in reserve in the Weikert woods near today's intersection of Hancock and United States avenues on Cemetery Ridge. Moved to the front of McGilvery's artillery line on the repulse of Pickett's Charge. Helped collect prisoners and tend to the wounded. Skirmishers reoccupied the fields belonging to the A. Trostle farm.

Report: On the morning of July 3, the regiment, pursuant to orders, constructed breastworks immediately in front of its line. The severe and long-continued artillery fire which the rebels opened upon us prior to their fruitless attack upon our position in the afternoon of this day, did no harm to any one in the regiment.

Colonel Roberts was killed while bravely leading on his men at the commencement of the action on July 2. The conduct of officers and men in these engagements at Gettysburg deserves the highest praise.

3rd CITATION, JULY 3RD: 88th Infantry.

GENERAL INFORMATION & DATA: See July 1st.

MONUMENT LOCATION: Ziegler's Grove. **MAP NO:** V, A-5.

SUMMARY: Held their position in Zeigler's Grove as indicated by their markers. Forced to move during the great cannonade. Moved south toward the Bryan farm on Pickett's repulse, continuing over the Emmitsburg Road. Assigned picket duty west of the Road. Several casualties reported while on this line facing the sunken Long Lane. Engaged in skirmishing throughout the night of July 3rd. Held their position throughout July 4th, the skirmishers still active to the west. Held this position on July 5th, men detailed to bury dead and collect arms. One detail was sent to Oak Rdge in search for information about their missing from the battle on the 1st.

July 3rd.

2ND CITATION, JULY 3RD: 107th Infantry.

GENERAL INFORMATION & DATA: See July 1st.

MONUMENT LOCATION: Ziegler's Grove. **MAP NO:** V, A-5.

SUMMARY: Held the position indicated by their monument north of the Bryan farm in Zeigler's Grove. Exposed to an incessant fire from enemy sharpshooters throughout their stay. Forced to change position during the great cannonade, moved deeper into Zeigler's Grove toward the Taneytown Road. Advanced back through the woods on Pickett's repulse. Lightly engaged as they collected prisoners and assumed picket duty west of the Emmitsburg Road. Skirmished throughout the night of July 3rd. Held their position in Zeigler's Grove until July 5th. Details formed to bury dead and collect arms. Moved south toward the Sherfy Peach Orchard on July 6th before proceeding toward Maryland.

Report: July 3.—At 4.30 a.m. we were posted in the rear of Cemetery Hill, in support of the batteries stationed on that point, remaining in that position until 1.30 p.m., when the enemy opened upon us with a heavy and furious artillery fire. Our division was moved to the right of Cemetery Hill, at the same time lying under two direct fires of the enemy's sharpshooters and one battery. The strife became terrific and the artillery firing terrible. At this crisis our services were required to support the batteries, when the regiment was marched with others along the crest or brow of the hill in rear of the batteries, through the most deadly fire ever man passed through, it appearing as though every portion of the atmosphere contained a deadly missile. After our services were no longer needed to support the batteries, the division to which my regiment was attached was moved to the left of Cemetery Hill, to participate in crowning our arms with the glorious victory achieved that day. My strength was about 72 guns and 11 commissioned officers. The day being very hot, 3 of my men were carried insensible from the field on account of the intense heat. After resting a few hours, we sent out a line of skirmishers to the front, and threw up breastworks to protect the men in our position, where we remain for the night. *July* 4.—We lay all day in the position of the previous night and strengthened it; did some skirmishing with the enemy's sharpshooters; had no casualties. It is proper here for me to state that the officers and men displayed great gallantry and determination throughout all the engagements of the previous days, and are entitled to the praise and gratitude of a free and loyal people.

SECOND CITATION, JULY 3RD: 110th Infantry.

GENERAL INFORMATION & DATA: See July 2.

MONUMENT LOCATION: See July 2. **MAP:** Not applicable.

SUMMARY: As ordered, the 110th was detached from its brigade early on July 3rd and moved to south Cemetery Hill where it went into position on the left of Maj. Osborne's artillery line above the Taneytown Road. Moved to various positions along this line, took several casualties during the cannonade. Moved forward on Pickett's repulse to a position along the Emmitsburg Road. Held this position throughout the night of July 3rd, returned to De Trobriand's brigade on July 4th, posted near the position of today's Pennsylvania Monument. Moved with the brigade toward the Wheatfield in search of their wounded and dead from the fighting on the 2nd. Helped bury the dead throughout the Wheatfield, Rose Woods and Stony Hill.

Report: Early on the morning of the 3d, I was ordered to move a short distance to the right, behind a piece of woods and near corps headquarters. After being in this position forty minutes, I was ordered to take up a position on the same ground occupied by this regiment the day before, previous to going into action.

At 1.30 p.m. I was ordered to move forward to a stone fence. Soon after being in this position, I was ordered to

July 3rd.

change position, and was conducted to the right, behind a battery, where I remained during the afternoon. The fire of the artillery was kept up all afternoon. At 8 p.m. I was ordered to move forward to act as a picket during the night, which was done. Here we remained until morning behind temporary earthworks. My command behaved well during the two days' battle, and as all did well and deserve praise, I will not particularly speak of any one.

SECOND CITATION, JULY 3RD: 2nd Cavalry.

GENERAL INFORMATION & DATA: See July 2.

MONUMENT LOCATION: See July 2nd. **MAP:** V, B-6.

SUMMARY: Served throughout the battlefield delivering orders as aides, couriers, and orderlies. During Pickett's Charge the men on hand at Army Headquarters were formed dismounted in line of battle and moved toward the crest of Cemetery Ridge. Held in reserve with several individual troopers continuing over the crest to engage the enemy at the Angle and Copse of Trees. Numerous casualties reported, none fatal. On the evening of the 3rd the entire regiment was recalled and escorted over 3,000 prisoners to Westminster, Maryland.

2ND CITATION, JULY 3RD: 1st Cavalry.

GENERAL INFORMATION & DATA: See July 2.

MONUMENT LOCATION: See July 2nd. **MAP:** V, B-5.

SUMMARY FOR JULY 3RD: Served as Army and Corps Headquarter escorts. Several squads detached to serve with the Provost Marshall on July 3rd. Most of the regiment was in reserve near Army Headquarters at the Leister House. Moved dismounted to the east brow of Cemetery Ridge. Formed in line of battle during Pickett's Charge, did not engage as one unit. Many individual troopers continued to the crest and helped in the Confederate repulse at the Copse of Trees.   Assisted in the rounding-up and guarding of prisoners from Pickett's Charge. Held position unitl July 5th when it rejoined Macintosh's brigade. Several companies detached to accompany prisoners to Westminster, Maryland.

2ND CITATION, JULY 3RD: 115th Infantry.

GENERAL INFORMATION & DATA: See July 2.

MONUMENT LOCATION: None. **MAP:** Not applicable.

SUMMARY: Supported the batteries along McGilvery's artillery line. Participated in the repulse of Pickett's Charge by moving to the right, following Kemper's line as it continued north toward the Copse of Trees.   Assisted in collecting prisoners from various Alabama, Florida, and Virginia regiments in front of the artillery line in the vicinity of today's Pennsylvania monument. Held this position for the remainder of the battle. Detailed to bury dead and burn captured and disabled weapons.

3rd CITATION, JULY 3RD: 1st Light, Battery B. (Cooper).

GENERAL INFORMATION & DATA: See July 2.

MONUMENT LOCATION: Incorrectly located along Hancock Avenue near today's Pennsylvania Monument. The correct position should be at the position indicated by Clark's 1st New Jersey Light, Battery B, several hundred yards south. **MAP:** V, G-5.

SUMMARY: At approximately 3:30 P.M. Cooper moved from the Artillery Park to McGilvery's line on Cemetery Ridge. Engaged in counter battery fire and also against Wilcox's and Lang's brigades, as they attacked the Federal line a few moments after Pickett's lines disapeared north. Instrumental in the repulse of this column. Held this position until July 5th.

July 3rd.

2ND CITATION, JULY 3RD: 119th Infantry.

GENERAL INFORMATION & DATA: See July 2.

MONUMENT LOCATION: Big Round Top. **MAP:** III, F-5.

SUMMARY: Early in the morning the regiment was marched to the left-center of the Federal line, going into position somewhere near today's Pennsylvania Monument. Immediately ordered to the crest of Big Round Top to the position indicated by its monument. One casualty from a Confederate sharpshooter. Held this position until July 5th.

2ND CITATION, JULY 3RD: 118th Infantry.

GENERAL INFORMATION & DATA: See July 2.

MONUMENT LOCATION: Big Round Top. **MAP:** III, F-5.

SUMMARY: Moved to this position early in the morning. Two men killed by enemy sharpshooter, otherwise not engaged. Held this position until July 5th.

2ND CITATION, JULY 3RD: 139th Infantry.

GENERAL INFORMATION & DATA: See July 2.

MONUMENT LOCATION: In center of Sherfy Peach Orchard north of Wheatfield Road on Sickles Ave. **MAP:** IV, E-7.

SUMMARY: At approximately 6:00 p.m. the regiment advanced west from its position along the Jacob Weikert farm lane into the Trostle woods, driving the few remaining enemy riflemen before them. Emerging at the stone wall that separates the Trostle woods from the fields east of the Emmitsburg Road, they received a well-directed volley from the enemy picket line posted in the Sherfy Peach Orchard. On orders the 139th advanced over the wall with the 6th Pennsylvania Reserves, driving the enemy back toward and over the Emmitsburg Road. Advanced to the high ground in the Peach Orchard and formed line of battle, skirmishing with enemy riflemen now posted west of the Emmitsburg Road. Darkness stopped the fight as the 139th held the position indicated by its monument. Pickets were sent to the Emmitsburg Road as the balance of the regiment returned to the position of their monument at the Jacob Weikert farm. Held this position until July 5th. Pickets actively engaged throughout the night of July 3rd. Details formed to bury dead and destroy captured and disabled arms.

2ND CITATION, JULY 3RD: 93rd Infantry.

GENERAL INFORMATION & DATA: See July 2.

MONUMENT LOCATION: None. **MAP:** Not applicable.

SUMMARY: At approximately 6:00 p.m. the 93rd advanced with the 139th Pa. Regiment into the Trostle woods, meeting little resistance, driving the few enemy riflemen before them. Moved with the 6th Reserves west of Plum Run and continued on to the rock wall separating the Trostle woods from the fields east of the Emmitsburg Road. Held this position and covered the 139th as they crossed over and continued into the Peach Orchard. At night the 93rd was pulled back to the Weikert farm, leaving a small picket line at the rock wall to support the 139th and 6th Reserves. Held their position in the Jacob Weikert farm yard until July 5th. Details formed to bury dead and destroy captured and disabled weapons.

UNIT: 102nd Infantry (mixed detachment of 10 men from each company). **OTHER NAME:** None.

ORGANIZATION: VI Corps, 3rd Div., 3rd Brig.

RAISED: From the counties of Lancaster and Philadelphia. **MUSTERED:** Pittsburg, Aug. 16,1861

COMMANDER: Lt. Robert W. Lyons (1842-1904).

July 3rd.

MONUMENT LOCATION: Just a few feet south of the Jacob Weikert farm above the sunken road. **MAP:** IV, J-3.

STRENGTH: 103 effectives. **LOSSES:** None.

WEAPONS: .58 Springfields & .69 Smoothbores.

SUMMARY: 100 men plus officers arrived on the field from detached guard duty with a wagon train on the morning of July 3rd. As ordered they took position behind the rock wall above the Jacob Weikert farm lane on the left of the 98th Pa. Not engaged. Held this position until July 5th. Detailed to bury dead and destroy captured arms.

2ND CITATION, JULY 3RD: 11th Reserves.

GENERAL INFORMATION & DATA: See July 2.

MONUMENT LOCATION: See July 2nd. **MAP:** Not applicable.

SUMMARY: The 11th advanced at approximately 6:00 p.m. moving from the stone wall east of their monument into the Wheatfield, west, toward the Stoney Hill, their right flank brushing the Trostle woods as they crossed the Wheatfield Road. Covered on their right by the 6th Reserves in the Trostle woods, the 11th advanced briskly, taking little fire from their front. Charged up and over the Stoney Hill meeting no resistance as the enemy in large numbers withdrew without firing a shot. Moved into the Peach Orchard driving rear-guard skirmishers back over the Emmitsburg Road. Held this position until July 5th with their skirmishers well west of the Emmitsburg Road.

Guide To Pennsylvania Troops

2ND CITATION, JULY 3RD: 1st Reserves.

GENERAL INFORMATION & DATA: See July 2.

MONUMENT LOCATION: None. **MAP:** Not applicable.

SUMMARY: At approximately 6:00 p.m., jumped over the low stone wall east of, and charged past their present day monument into the bloody Wheatfield, continuing west to the top of the Stoney Hill. Reformed their lines and charged into the Peach Orchard, driving large enemy numbers before them. Captured one disabled enemy 12-pounder Napoleon belonging to a battery that withdrew as they closed on it. Went into position in the Peach Orchard with skirmishers west of the Emmitsburg Road. Pickets posted well west of the Peach Orchard kept up a continuous fire into the night of July 3rd. Held their position until July 5th. Details were sent back to the Wheatfield and Valley of Death to bury their dead.

2ND CITATION, JULY 3RD: 2nd Reserves.

GENERAL INFORMATION & DATA: See July 2.

MONUMENT LOCATION: See July 2nd. **MAP:** Not applicable.

SUMMARY: At approximately 6:00 p.m. the 2nd advanced from the stone wall east of their monument charging into the Wheatfield toward the the Rose Woods. The right companies skirted the edge of the wheatfield, following north of a stone wall and west toward the marshy low ground, as the center and left wings entered the woods south of the same wall. Heavy enemy resistance was met as the Confedetares attempted to hold a rock and wood reinforced fence mid-way into the Rose Woods. The enemy, hit from the north by enfilading fire from the 1st Reserves on the Stoney Hill, gave way moving back toward the Plum Run and Rose farm, pressed closely by the 2nd. Another attempt by the enemy to check the 2nd's advance at the wood fence bordering the

July 3rd.

Rose farm was foiled as their left regiments pulled out of line without engaging. Over 200 prisoners were rounded up as the 2nd moved along the fence line from the north, eventually joining the 13th Reserves in the Rose Meadows. Ended this engagement on the Emmitsburg Road with skirmishers moving west toward Warfield Ridge. Held their position near the Emmitsburg Road until July 5th. Details formed to bury their dead in the Wheatfield and Valley of Death.

2ND CITATION, JULY 3RD: 9th Reserves.

GENERAL INFORMATION & DATA: See July 2.

MONUMENT LOOCATION: See July 2. **MAP:** Not applicable.

SUMMARY: At approximately 6:00 p.m. the regiment advanced from its position on Little Round Top, indicated by its monument, moving west into the Valley of Death supporting the 10th Reserves on its left flank. Moved onto Houck's Ridge collecting prisoners and arms. One casualty wounded by a enemy sharpshooter. Returned to position on Little Round Top. Held in reserve at this position until July 5th. Detailed to bury dead and destroy captured arms.

2ND CITATION, JULY 3RD: 10th Reserves.

GENERAL INFORMATION & DATA: See July 2.

MONUMENT LOCATION: See July 2. **MAP:** III, D-6.

SUMMARY: At about 6:00 p.m. the regiment advanced across the Valley of Death from the saddle between the Round Tops, collecting 1,000 stands of arms and over 200 prisoners. Skirmishers continued west into the Rose woods driving the few remaining enemy riflemen before them. All five of the regiment's casualties occurred during this operation. Aside from a detail of pickets, the regiment returned to its position until July 5th held in reserve.

Guide To Pennsylvania Troops

SECOND CITATION, JULY 3RD: 27th Infantry.

GENERAL INFORMATION & DATA: See July 2.

MONUMENT LOCATION: See July 2nd. **MAP:** VII, A-3.

SUMMARY: Held the same position as on the evening of July 2nd indicated by their monument on East Cemetery Hill. Actively engaged with enemy sharpshooters posted in houses 200 yards to their front. Skirmishers at the north base of Cemetery Hill moved out to positions well in advance of their main line in the houses and yards as far north as today's Breckenridge Avenue. The balance of the regiment lay in reserve in rear the stonewall atop East Cemetery Hill. Subjected to terrible sharpshooting and artillery cross-fire that passed overhead doing little physical damage. No casualties reported on July 3rd, as well as limited engagement. Held this position until July 4th when the regiment moved into town. Posted on July 5th somewhere along the Baltimore Pike north of their present day monument. Details were formed to bury dead and search for missing and wounded from their battle on July 1st.

2ND CITATION, JULY 3RD: 3rd Cavalry.

GENERAL INFORMATION & DATA: See July 2nd.

MONUMENT: East Cavalry field. **Map:** VII, E-3 & F-4.

SUMMARY: Arrived on East Cavalry Battlefield at about 1:00 p.m. with McIntosh's brigade via the fields and farmlanes toward the Low Dutch Road, approximately 2 miles due east of their previous position near Cress Ridge. The 3rd was placed on the far right flank of of the Federal line facing the Rummel Farm and fields. Dismounted skirmishers advanced and annoyed the Confederate skirmishers to the point that a Confederate mounted charge was thrown against their small numbers. One Michigan regiment counter-charged the Confederates, helping to check the enemy attack for a few moments, allowing the 3rd regiment skirmishers retired

July 3rd.

into some woods where reinforcements waited. With the Michigan regiment beaten back, the Confederates renewed their mounted attack against the 3rd Cavalry in the fields and woods several hundred yards west of today's Gregg Avenue. A counter-charge by a small detachment of the 3rd hit the Confederates head on as dismounted troopers from the 3rd converged on their flanks. Overpowering numbers stopped the Confederate charge as the detachment from the 3rd cut their way through the enemy line, only to be cut off themselves. Fighting their way out in hand to hand combat while mounted, most of the mounted troopers returned to the area near thier present day monument along Gregg Avenue. Dismounted skirmishers again moved out of the woods toward the Rummel farm keeping the enemy at bay for the rest of the afternoon. Held this position until July 5th with small detachments scowering the nearby countryside for enemy troop movement.

UNIT: 61st Infantry. **OTHER NAME:** None.

ORGANIZATION: VI Corps, 2nd Div., 3rd Brig.

RAISED: from the counties of Allegheney, Luzerne, & Philadelphia. **MUSTERED:** Camp Copeland, Pittsburgh, Aug. 13, 1861.

COMMANDER: Lt. Col. George F. Smith, 1840-1877.

MONUMENT LOCATION: Located on Neil Ave., the least visited and best kept secret in all of the Gettysburg National Military Park. Approximately 800 yards due east of the old (G.Hokes) Toll House, itself located on the east shoulder of the Baltimore Pike, just south of the Rock Creek bridge. Easy access is by way of the Clapsaddle Road, via Highland Avenue. Represents the position held by the regiment on 3rd, and the extreme right flank of the Army of the Potomac's infantry line. **Map:** VI, J-8.

STRENGTH: 10 Cos, 386 Effectives. **LOSSES:** K-0, W-1, M-1. Total: 2. Percent Loss: .5

WEAPONS: .58 Springfields.

SUMMARY: After a grueling march from Maryland the regiment reached the battlefield in the late afternoon of July 2nd, resting for the night near Rock Creek. Not engaged. Near dawn on the 3rd, moved due east toward heavy woods several hundred yards east of the Baltimore Pike. Went into position on the right flank of Neil's brigade facing due north at the position indicated by their present monument. Skirmishers sent forward made immediate contact with Confederate pickets who opened on them with sporadic but accurate fire. Held this position throughout the day. A lively fight ensued at approximately 2:00 P.M. when portions of Walker's Virginia Brigade, on a reconoiter in force, ran into Neil's skirmishers, including those from the 61st. Skirmishing was kept up into the evening and night of July 3rd. The 61st skirmishers also made contact with dismounted Federal vedettes from the 16th Pennsylvania Cavalry off their right flank near the intersection of Highland and Clapssaddle Avenues. The 16th also became engaged when Walker's skirmishers attempted to move around the 61st's right flank. The 61st held this position unitl July 5th. No further engagement reported.

2ND CITATION, JULY 3RD: Independent Battery E. (Atwell).

GENERAL INFORMATION & DATA: See July 2nd.

MONUMENT LOCATION: See July 2nd.

SUMMARY: Opened at heavy cannonade from their position on Powers Hill to that of the enemy on the lower reaches of Culps Hill, approximately 800 yards northeast. Numerous shells from this battery exploded above the ranks of Colgrove's brigade causing several fatal casualties. Not until a note from the commanding officer of the 2nd Massachusetts Regiment threatning Atwell with a charge, did the battery elevate its guns and change direction of fire. Continued to fire onto Culp's Hill untill about 10:00 A.M. Opened again during the great cannonade to the east toward enemy position east of Rock Creek. This action lasted approximately fifteen minutes. One half battery was ordered to Cemetery Ridge on the repulse of Pickett's Charge, taking a position at the Angle previously occupied by Cushing's 4th U.S. Battery A. Returned to Powers Hill on July 4th, holding this position until July 5th.

2ND CITATION, JULY 3RD: 49th Infantry.

GENERAL INFORMATION & DATA: See July 2nd.

MONUMENT LOCATION: None.

SUMMARY FOR JULY 3RD: At approximately 4:00 P.M. the regiment was moved from their position along today's Howe Avenue toward the Copse of Trees. On reaching the approximate position of the Hummelbaugh farm lane the regiment was ordered to the left to support the troops on Big Round Top. Arrived on Big Round Top and went into position near the 119th Pa. Infantry. Held their position on or near Big Round Top until July 5th.

2ND CITATION, JULY 3RD: 16th Cavalry.

GENERAL INFORMATION & DATA: See July 2nd.

MONUMENT LOCATION: See July 2nd. **MAP:** VII, E-8.

SUMMARY: Spent all the morning and early afternoon on picket duty east of Rock Creek with skirmishers and vendetts posted throughout the lanes and woods in the area south of Wolf's Hill. Made contact with Walkers Virginia Brigade as enemy skirmishers moved south through the woods toward present day Clapsaddle Avenue. Opened a brisk fire on the small enemy line driving the Rebels back with superior firepower with their carbines. Two men killed during this engagement. The left flank of the 16th's skirmishers linked up with the right of the 61st Pennsylvania Infantry, solidifying that part of the Federal line and discouraging any further Confederate movement against that part of the line. Held this line until July 5th when the regiment returned to Gregg's brigade. Spent most of July 4th and 5th as vendetts throughout the Wolf Hill area.

2ND CITATION, JULY 3RD: 6th Cavalry.

GENERAL INFORMATION & DATA: See July 2..

MONUMENT LOCATION: See July 2nd. **MAP NO:**
SUMMARY FOR JULY 3RD: Two companies continued to serve at Army Headquarters doing excellent service throughout the battlefield. Several troopers stayed on at Army Headquarters when it was abandoned during the great cannonade. Some mounted troopers rode over the crest of Cemetery Ridge without orders offering their services to officers at the Copse of Trees. All casualties reported were during the cannonade and Pickett's Charge. Held their position with Headquarters until July 5th.

UNIT: 18th Cavalry. **OTHER NAME:** "163rd Volunteers".

ORGANIZATION: Cavalry Corps, 3rd Div., 1st Brig.

RAISED: From the Counties of Allegheny, Cambria, Crawford, Dauphin, Greene, Lycoming, Philadelphia, & Washington.
MUSTERED: Camp Curtin, Harrisburg, Nov., 1862

COMMANDER: Lt. Col. William P. Brinton, 1832-1881-?

July 3rd.

(Reported missing in Argentina).

MONUMENT LOCATION: Above the south shoulder of West Confederate Avenue at the base of Big Round Top (Also monuments at Hanover for June 30th & Hunterstown for July 2nd). **MAP:** III, G-1.

STRENGTH: 12 Cos, 258 effectives. **LOSSES:** K-3, W-8, M-4. Total: 15. Percent Loss: 6.

WEAPONS: Burnside Carbines, Colt .44s.

SUMMARY: After participating in the repulse of the Confederate cavalry at Hanover on June 30th, the regiment proceeded toward Gettysburg after one day's rest. Held in reserve during the cavalry action at Hunterstown on July 2nd. Continued to Gettysburg arriving mid-morning on July 3rd. Moved south around Big Round Top, with the brigade, to cover the army's left flank. Led by Brig. Gen. Elon G. Farnsworth, on orders from Brig. Gen. Judson Kirkpatrick, the regiment charged north from the position of their present-day monument on West Confederate Avenue, in a desperate but futile mounted attack against Confederate infantry entrenched behind stone and rail fences, aided by a heavily wooded area, below the northwest base of Big Round Top. Repulsed with casualties. The regiment returned to the position indicated by their monument and held this position until July 4th.

Guide To Pennsylvania Troops

Select Bibliography

Bachelder, John H. *Official Battlefield Maps Of Gettysburg.* Washington, D.C.: Office of the U. S. Army Chief of Engineer, 1876.

Bates, Samuel P. *History Of The Pennsylvania Volunteers, 1861-1865.* Vol. I - IV. Reprint of 1870 edition. Wilmington, N.C.: Broadfoot Publishing, 1993.

Busey, John. W. *These Honored Dead.* Hightstown, N.J.: Longstreet House, 1986.

Busey, John W., and Martin, David G. *Regimental Strengths And Losses At Gettysburg.* Hightstown, N.J.: Longstreet House, 1986.

Coddington, Edwin. *The Gettysburg Campaign.* Dayton: Morningside Books, 1968.

Frassanito, William. *Early Photography At Gettysburg.* Gettysburg: Thomas Publications, 1995.

Ladd, David and Audrey, eds. *The Bachelder Papers.* Vol. I - III. Dayton, Ohio: Morningside Books, 1994-5.

Martin, David G. *Gettysburg: July 1st.* Philadelphia: Combined Books, 1995.

Pfanz, Harry W. *Gettysburg: The Second Day.* Chapel Hill, N.C.: University of North Carolina Press, 1987.

Pfanz Harry W. *Gettysburg: Culp's Hill And Cemetery Hill.* Chapel Hill, N.C.: University of North Carolina Press, 1994.

Raus, Edmund J. *A Generation On The March: The Union Army At Gettysburg.* Lynchburg, VA.: H.E. Howard, Inc.

Ray, William S. *Pennsylvania At Gettysburg: Ceremonies At*

176

July 3rd.

The Dedication Of The Monuments Erected By The Commonwealth. Vol., I-III. Harrisburg: Commonwealth of Pennsylvania, 1914.

Report Of The Select Committee Relative To The Soldiers' National Cemetery. Harrisburg, PA: The Commonwealth of Pennsylvania, 1864-1867. Gettysburg: Thomas Publications.

Rollins, Richard, ed. *Pickett's Charge: Eyewitness Accounts.* Redondo Beach, California: Rank and File Publications, 1994.

Sauers, Richard A., Comp. *Advance The Colors!: Pennsylvania Civil War Battle Flags.* Vol. I. Harrisburg, Pa.: Capitol Preservation Committee, 1987.

Stewart, George. *Pickett's Charge: A Microhistory Of The Final Attack At Gettysburg, July 3, 1863.* Boston: Houghton-Mifflin, 1959.

Taylor, Frank H. *Philadelphia In The Civil War.* Philadelphia: City of Philadelphia, 1913.

Tucker, Glen. *High Tide At Gettysburg.* Dayton: Morningside Books, 1987.

Walters, Sara G. *Inscription At Gettysburg.* Gettysburg, PA: Thomas Publications 1991.

U.S. War Department. *War Of The Rebellion. Official Records Of The Union And Confederate Armies.* Series I. Vol. XXVII. Parts I &. III. Washington: Government Printing Office. 1889-1901.

Walker, Francis A. *History Of The Second Army Corps.* New York.: Chas. Scribner &. Sons, 1887.

Congressional Medal of Honor
Awarded to Men from Pennsylvania Regiments.

For Action on July 1st.

1). 88th Regiment. First Sgt. Edward L. Gilligan for capturing a Confederate flag on Oak Ridge, while engaged in hand to hand combat.

2). 90th Regiment. Maj. Alfred J. Sellers. Assumed command of the regiment on the field of battle on Oak Ridge after its commanding officer was shot. Personally led the 90th on two counter-attacks and successfully withdrew his unit from the field, partially covering the I &. XI Corps retreat as they fled through town to Cemetery Hill.

3). 143rd Regiment. Sgt. James M. Rutter of Company C assisted his wounded Captain from the McPherson farm at great risk, and carried him to safety in Gettysburg, while under extreme musketry fire and demands to surrender.

4). 150th Regiment. Lt. Col. Henry S. Huidekoper. After being shot in the right arm during a counter-charge against the railroad cut, assumed command of the regiment and led his right wing back to the McPherson farm to join the left, where they continued to hold their position in the farm lane facing due west, against three assaults from Brockenbrough's Virginia Brigade.

5). 150th Regiment. Corporal Monroe J. Reisinger of Company H. For bravery beyond the call of duty and for meritorious conduct while in the face of the enemy.

For action on July 2nd.

6 - 11). 6th Reserves. Sgt. Wallace W. Johnson, Co. G., Sgt. John W. Hart, Co. D., Sgt. George W. Mear's, Co. A., Corp. J. L. Roush, Co. D., Corp. Chester S. Furman, Co. A., and

July 3rd.

Pvt. Thaddeus S. Stevens, Co. E. All six men volunteered and left their ranks below south Cemetery Ridge, and while under heavy rifle and musketry, attacked Confederate sharpshooters posted in the Jacob Weikert farmhouse.

12). 26th Regiment. Sgt. George W. Roosevelt of Co. K., for the capture of a Confederate flag on July 2, during hand to hand combat east of the Emmitsburg Road, across from the Rogers house. Roosevelt was severely wounded and nearly captured.

13). 99th Regiment. Color Sgt. Harvey M. Munsell, Co A., led his regiment up the Valley of Death in a desperate attempt to stop the Confederate attack against Devil's Den and Houck's Ridge. The regiment wheeled right and Munsell took the colors up to the top of Houck's Ridge where he planted his flag near Smith's N.Y. battery. The regiment responded by rallying on the colors. In time Munsell and the 99th were forced off the ridge with all other Federal units, and pulled back to Cemetery Ridge. Munsell also carried the colors with distinction on July 3rd.

14). Independent Batteries C & F. Consolidated. Pvt. Casper Carlisle, of Co. F with only two wheel horses harnessed to his limber, one mortally wounded, and with Capt. James Thompson, the battery commander, tugging on its bridle, Pvt. Carlisle pulled his rifled cannon away from the Wheatfield Road in the Peach Orchard, and certain capture. Fired on from three sides, Carlisle and Capt. Thompson nursed the dying horse along, north past Bigalow's 9th Mass. battery as it prolonged back toward the Trostle farm. Carlisle reached the Trostle gate at the lane, where the wounded horse dropped dead. Aided by another caisson driver, Carlisle hitched two replacement horses to his limber and pulled his gun east over Plum Run and into McGilvery's new artillery line.

15). 140th Infantry. Sgt. James Pipes of Co.A., for action on July 2nd, after he was seriously wounded in the back while rescuing a downed comrade in a exposed field, and carrying him to safety under extreme enemy fire.

16). 140th Infantry. Lt. James J. Purman of Co. A., for helping Sgt. Pipes, of his company, rescue a wounded comrade from a bullet - swept field. Although severely shot in the left leg, Lt. Purman continued to carry the stricken soldier through the lines where he collapsed from loss of blood. Purman's left leg was amputated above the knee on July 3rd.

For Action on July 3rd.

17). 3rd Cavalry. Capt. William E. Miller of Co. H., without orders, led a charge on the enemy's left flank, disrupting a planned charge and checking their advance, driving them back past the Rummel farm. Miller's squadron was nearly cut off after driving into the enemy line. Refusing to surrender, Miller turned about and hacked his way back to the main Federal line near the Low Dutch Road.

18). 1st Reserves. Sgt. James B. Thompson, of Co. G., for his action on July 3rd near the Emmitsburg Road. After Pickett's repulse, some V Corps units advanced through the Rose woods toward the Emmitsburg Road. In heavy fighting Thompson captured the flag of the 15th Georgia.

19). 71st Regiment. Pvt. John E. Clopp of Co. F, for the capture of the 9th Virginia flag during Pickett's Charge on July 3rd. He was seen by many wrestling with the color bearer amongst Cushing's wrecked battery east of the rock wall.

Errata

p. xix: 84th monument is south of 8th Cavalry monument.
p. 3: 26th Militia's monument at intersection of Chambersburg Pike and Fairfield Road.

< p. 7: 56th monument July 1st.

p.16: Monument for >
Cooper's battery >
on July 1st. >

p. 21: 150th on July 1st. >

< p. 21: 74th on July 1st.

p. 85: Ind. Batt. C is Thompson's.
p.101: 69th monument is 280' west of Hancock Ave.

p. 112: 107th on July 2,3. >

p. 125: Incorrect photo for 56th(monument missing).
p. 147: For information on 151st, see July 1st.
p. 157: For information on 143rd, 149th and 150th, see July 1st.

p. 157: 143rd monument. >

< p. 157: 149th monument.

p. 157: 150th monument. >

< p. 164: Cooper's battery.

Note: 84th Infantry, 12th Reserves and 8th Cavalry were not significantly engaged.

UNIT: 13th Reserves. **OTHER NAME:** "42nd Infantry," "1st Bucktails," "1st Rifles."

ORGANIZATION: V Corps, 3rd Div., 1st Brig. **RAISED:** From the counties of Cameron, Carbon, Chester, Clearfield, Elk, McKean, Perry, Tioga, & Warren. **MUSTERED:** Camp Curtin, Harrisburg. Fall of 1862. **COMMANDER:** Lt. Col. Charles F. Taylor (1840-1863). KIA on July 2nd. 2) Maj. Ross Hartshorne (1839-1905).

MONUMENT LOCATION: Inside the loop of Ayres Ave., atop north Houcks Ridge, approximately 75 yards east of the intersection of Ayres and Sickles Avenues. 2) A memorial marker to Col. Taylor, located on the north shoulder of Ayres Ave. just inside the woods east of the Wheatfield.

STRENGTH: 10 Cos, 297 Effectives. **LOSSES:** K- 7, W-39, M-2. Total: 48, Percent Loss: 16.2. **WEAPONS:** .577 Enfields, .69 smoothbores & Sharps Rifles.

SUMMARY: Advanced with the brigade from north of the Little Round Top west, toward the Wheatfield, 700 yards distant. The 13th was ordered farther to the left and obliqued south toward Houck's Ridge in order to address the enfilading fire coming from the Rose woods. Passing over at a slight left angle to Crawford Ave., they continued across the Valley of Death to the west-southwest, passing today's marker to Smith's New York section just west of Crawford Ave. Climbing east Houck's Ridge between the saddles, they drove into the woods forcing back the remaining Confederates. Ordered forward to reconnoiter, Taylor was shot near his present memorial marker. The regiment held this line indicated by its monument for the remainder of the battle.

2ND CITATION, JULY 2ND: 143rd, 149th, & 150th Infantry.

GENERAL INFORMATION & DATA: See July 1st.

MONUMENT LOCATIONS: All three monuments are on the east shoulder of Hancock Ave., approximately 250-300 yards south of the Copse of Trees on Cemetery Ridge.

SUMMARY FOR JULY 2ND: All three regiments moved from near Ziegler's Grove to a position indicated by their monuments. The 143rd and 149th were lightly engaged while holding their position atop the ridge. The 150th followed the Federal counter-charge to the Emmitsburg Road, collecting prisoners and two abandoned 12-pounder Napoleons. The 150th returned to the line held by the 143rd & 149th with their trophies.